ROMANCE BEHIND JUDAICA

Celebrating the Richness of the Jewish Calendar

FAYDRA L. SHAPIRO *with* LEN WOODS

WORTHY®

New York • Nashville

Worthy
Hachette Book Group
1290 Avenue of the Americas, New York, NY 10104

worthypublishing.com
twitter.com/worthypub

First Edition: August 2019

Worthy is a division of Hachette Book Group, Inc. The Worthy name and logo are trademarks of Hachette Book Group, Inc.

The publisher is not responsible for websites (or their content) that are not owned by the publisher.

Cover design by Chris Gilbert, Studio Gearbox
Print book interior design by Peachtree Publishing Services

Cataloging-in-Publication Data is on file with the Library of Congress.

ISBNs: 978-1-9454-7038-7 (hardcover), 978-1-9454-7090-5 (ebook)

Printed in the United States of America
LSC-C

10 9 8 7 6 5 4 3 2 1

CONTENTS

INTRODUCTION

I f you were playing the word-association game and some-one said "holiday," what words or images would spring to mind? *Travel? Time off from work? Break from school?* Would you think *parties* or *dinners? Family* or *houseguests?*

Clearly the word *holiday* has broad connotations in contemporary culture. For many it means shopping, cleaning, cooking, decorating—and the very real possibili-ty of ending up far more stressed than rested. Your favorite holiday is probably a prime example. Think of how excited you are for the big day to arrive—and how relieved you are when it has finally passed!

Maybe we're celebrating holidays all wrong?

Perhaps we should consider the Jewish people and the calendar given to them by God in the Tanakh.[1] Woven into the weeks and seasons is an assortment of observances and traditions. Not the kind of *holidays* we moderns tend to practice, but *holy days*: blessed com-mandments to step away from the rush and tedium of everyday existence; sacred occasions for remembering, reflecting on, and rejoicing in ultimate realities; each festival a gracious invitation to reconnect with God and others;[2] each special day an opportunity to rekindle the God-given desire to be different and to make a difference in our broken world.

This is a book about those Jewish holidays.[3] In these pages we'll explore the mystery of Sabbath and the miracle of Passover. We'll examine the majesty of Yom Kippur, the mirth of Purim, and the rich meaning behind other observances. Even the more recent Jewish holidays *not* mentioned or mandated in the Bible have a compelling beauty and significance that few realize.

To assist us in our understanding, we'll rely on an old Jewish practice known as *hiddur mitzvah*.

The Torah says, "The LORD is my strength and my might, and he has become my salvation; this is my God, and *I will praise him*, my father's God, and *I will exalt him*" (Exodus 15:2, emphasis added).

The great Talmudic sage Rabbi Ishmael wrestled with the question of how finite humans can adequately praise and exalt an infinite Creator. He concluded that this is only possible by carrying out God's commandment (*mitzvah* in Hebrew) in glorious or beautiful (*hiddur* in Hebrew) ways. He therefore vowed to use only exquisite and costly ceremonial objects in worship: "I shall prepare before him a beautiful lulav, beautiful sukkah, beautiful fringes . . . and beautiful phylacteries."[4]

Hiddur mitzvah—this beautification in performing a commandment—applies to all sorts of ritual items connected with the holidays: the *sukkah* that Jews sit in and the *kiddush* cup Jews drink from, the spice box Jews smell and the *hagaddah* Jews read from. This ancient practice of hiddur mitzvah is the reason many Jewish families and congregations spare no expense in acquiring exquisite items for use in their holiday observances.

You don't know what those things are? No worries. By the end of this book you will.

THE SABBATH

A popular Jewish folktale says that when the ancient Israelites assembled at Mount Sinai, God offered them eternal life (*olam ha'ba*, "the world to come") if they would agree to keep his commandments. In response, the people asked the Almighty, "Before we decide, could you let us sample heaven first?"

God graciously consented to this bold request by giving the Israelites Shabbat (i.e., the Sabbath).[5]

According to the sages, this is how Shabbat came to be the central element of Jewish life, the foundation of the Jewish calendar. And it is why many Jews describe this weekly "island in time"[6] as "a taste of the world to come."[7]

The Sabbath

"More than Israel has kept the Sabbath, the Sabbath has

kept Israel."

—Ahad Ha'am

In 1979 an American dentist named Dave Baab moved
to Tel Aviv, Israel, to teach at a dental school. He and his
wife, Lynne, found a flat near the main highway leading
north out of the city. The location and price were right,
but the noise—they quickly discovered—was deafening.
Loud cargo trucks, thundering buses, and an unending
stream of honking motorists zoomed past their apartment
all hours of the day (and night).

Until the Sabbath.

Writing of their experience, Lynne describes the deafening silence that engulfed the Jewish section of the city
each week from Friday evening to Saturday evening. Buses
stopped running. Businesses and stores closed. "There
was simply nothing to do. . . . Life really did stop for us."[8]

Unsettling at first, the Sabbath and its quiet quickly became the Baabs' favorite part of each week. In fact, Lynne confesses, "As darkness fell on Saturday evening, we could hear the buses and trucks begin to rumble along the main road. With the noise came a sense of loss."[9]

The Origins of Sabbath

The idea of earmarking one day a week for stopping and being still can be traced back to the dawn of time. After describing the creation of the world in six days, the Torah says, "Thus the heavens and the earth were finished, and all their multitude. And on the seventh day God finished the work that he had done, and he rested on the seventh day from all the work that he had done. So God blessed the seventh day and hallowed it, because on it God rested from all the work that he had done in creation" (Genesis 2:1–3).

Though this passage doesn't contain the word *Sabbath*, it does contain the verb *rested*, which comes from the same Hebrew root word. Some have pointed out that the word *rested* seems to suggest that God found the work of creation taxing, if not exhausting. Jewish scholars and theologians scoff at such an idea by citing numerous other Bible passages that describe God's limitless power (e.g., Numbers 11:23; Jeremiah 32:17). They also point out that the Hebrew word translated *rested* in Genesis 2:2 literally means "to stop or desist from labor." In other words, they argue, God didn't quit creating in order to take a much-needed nap. He took a break from his creative endeavors to savor and enjoy the "very good" world he had made (Genesis 1:31).

By this act the Almighty set apart and "hallowed" (made holy) the seventh day. What's more, he infused his newly created world with a kind of work-rest rhythm. In short, the idea of Shabbat existed long before the Jewish nation existed, and certainly before the command "Remember the sabbath day, and keep it holy" (Exodus 20:8) was ever engraved on a tablet of Sinai stone.

The book of Exodus expands on this Sabbath principle. The Israelites, on their way to receive the Torah at Mount Sinai, were given a vivid lesson in laboring six days and ceasing their labors on the seventh. This les-

son came as Moses explained the miraculous "bread
from heaven" (v. 4) the people discovered at their feet
one morning while beginning their journey. What was
this "flaky substance, as fine as frost on the ground"
(v. 14)? "The house of Israel called it manna; it was
like coriander seed, white, and the taste of it was like
wafers made with honey" (v. 31).[10] "Six days you shall
gather it," Moses told the people, "but on the seventh
day, which is a sabbath, there will be none" (v. 26).

Despite this explicit warning, some Israelites went out
to gather manna on the seventh day and came back
empty-handed. (We can probably attribute their
behavior to the deeply ingrained habits of a people
only recently liberated from slavery—the idea of a
"day off" was foreign to them.) In any case, God
reminded the Israelites through Moses, "See! The
LORD has given you the sabbath, therefore on the
sixth day he gives you food for two days; each of you
stay where you are; do not leave your place on the seventh day. So the people rested on the seventh day"
(Exodus 16:29–30).

The Purpose of Sabbath

Misconceptions abound about the Jewish practice of Sabbath. To the uninformed, the very idea seems draconian: an

 The Jewish Understanding of Time

Norman Solomon has argued that if we suddenly found ourselves in a world without calendars and clocks, we'd have no choice but to measure time by nature. We'd dispense with the not entirely logical practice of beginning the new day at midnight (when most people are sleeping). Instead, we'd calculate days by either sunrises or sunsets. We'd measure months by watching the phases of the moon. We'd pay close attention to the four seasons (assuming we lived in regions that actually have four seasons).[11]

This is what the ancient people of Israel did. To measure days, they looked to the sun, deciding that a day ends when the sun *sets*—with the new day beginning immediately thereafter. They learned this practice from the story of creation, which explicitly marks the ending and beginning of each day in the exact same manner: "And there was evening, and there was morning, the first (second, third, etc.)

day." This is why Shabbat begins Friday evening—after sundown.

Likewise, to measure months, the people of Israel paid close attention to the moon. In fact, the ancient Hebrew word for "month" is *yerach*, which comes from *yareach*, the Hebrew word for "moon." And this brings us to Rosh Chodesh (literally "head of the month" or, in everyday vernacular, the "new moon"). In ancient times, Rosh Chodesh was an important holiday. As soon as the Jewish religious authorities confirmed that the crescent of a new moon was visible, this news was "announced" to the nation via a system of hilltop signal fires. At the temple, shofars (rams' horns) were blown and special sacrifices were made. Centuries later, when the temple was destroyed in 70 CE, Rosh Chodesh became a semi-festival, not forgotten but marked by a special public announcement of the coming month and additional prayers and Torah readings included in the regular liturgy.

In the fourth century CE, Rabbi Hillel II used basic astronomy and math to create a perpetual or fixed calendar. This eliminated the need for Jewish authorities to spend their time moon watching and dispatching messengers to notify the nation of the start of a new month.

entire day *every* week filled with stifling restrictions? Shabbat strikes many as, at best, a grim exercise in self-denial

 ## Why Do Jewish Holidays—Other Than the Sabbath—"Move" around the Calendar?

There are different kinds of calendars. The *solar* calendar (also known as the Gregorian or civil calendar) is built around the four distinct seasons and is determined by how long it takes the earth to revolve around the sun—about 365 days. The *lunar* calendar, on the other hand, is unrelated to the four seasons. It calculates months by how long it takes the moon to revolve around the earth—approximately 29.5 days. Do the math and you'll see that twelve lunar months make for a lunar year of only 354 days. Thus, with a lunar calendar, holidays come eleven days earlier each passing year. Islam follows a lunar calendar—which explains why in 2003 Ramadan began in late *October*, and why in 2022 Ramadan will begin in early *April*.

Since the Torah stipulates that the festival of Sukkot take place in the fall and that Passover be observed each spring, a strict lunar calendar was out of the question for the Jews. They solved this "solar vs.

and, at worst, a kind of divine chastisement—like being
grounded or put in time-out by the Almighty.

lunar" dilemma by creating a hybrid lunar-solar
calendar that recognizes both the seasons and
the monthly phases of the moon. To make it work
practically, they add a thirteenth (i.e., "leap") month
approximately every third year—and refer to these
years as "pregnant" because they are "bigger" years.

A short time later, when the Torah was given at
Sinai, this practice of setting aside a weekly day of
rest was formally demanded of God's people. It is a
mitzvah—a divine command to be carried out, not
an interesting theory to be discussed and debated.
Shabbat, as some have noted, is the only Jewish
holiday observance that made it into the Ten Commandments: "Remember the sabbath day, and
keep it holy. Six days you shall labor and do all your
work. But the seventh day is a sabbath to the LORD
your God; you shall not do any work—you, your son
or your daughter, your male or female slave, your
livestock, or the alien resident in your towns. For in
six days the LORD made heaven and earth, the sea,
and all that is in them, but rested the seventh day;
therefore the LORD blessed the sabbath day and
consecrated it" (Exodus 20:8–11).

But listen as observant Jews discuss their experience. They positively gush about the Sabbath's many delights. "Shabbat is like nothing else," writes Nan Fink, a midlife convert to Judaism. "Shabbat is a meditation of unbelievable beauty."[12] Rabbi Ted Falcon compares it to "a special guest who comes to visit each Friday night and stays until nightfall on Saturday. This guest is so full of grace and light, so loved and so loving, that to have her arrive is a pleasure and to see her leave brings sadness."[13] Rabbi Yitzchok Adlerstein likens the Sabbath to "a week in Hawaii without ever leaving home."[14] And in his classic book on the subject, Jewish theologian Abraham Joshua Heschel called the time from sunset on Friday to sundown on Saturday "the most precious present mankind has received from the treasure house of God."[15]

Why do practitioners of Shabbat rave about it so? For at least seven reasons:

1. Sabbath is a day of **rest**.

With the gift of Shabbat, God says to his people, in effect: "You've been scrambling and striving, creating and accomplishing for six straight days. Enough. Time for a

The Work Can Wait

After winning the 1951 Pulitzer Prize for *The Caine Mutiny*, Herman Wouk found himself adapting his acclaimed novel for the stage. In January of 1954, with the play's opening just two weeks away and the production mired in major rewrites, Wouk, an observant Jew, stunned his director. He announced on Friday afternoon that he was leaving the theater to observe Sabbath and that he would be back the following night.

The director came unglued. He reminded the author that time was running out—they couldn't afford to lose an entire day. Investors had put hundreds of thousands of dollars into the project. The actors were still waiting for a finished script. "I'm sorry," Wouk replied, "but my religious commitments are more important to me than revising the play."

Wouk departed. When he returned on Saturday night, the tension in the theatre was palpable. Wouk, however, was rested and refreshed. Able to see the script's flaws with a new perspective, he quickly solved them.[16]

much-needed break. Stop all you're doing and simply *be*.
Turn off your smartphones. Lose your to-do lists and relax.
On this day, I want you catching your breath—and perhaps
a few extra z's. I want you to trust me—that even as *you* go
off duty, *I* will continue running the universe. I have everything under control—this big, wide world and your mysterious, messy life too."

This commitment to a day of rest is perhaps best pictured in
an old *New Yorker* cartoon that shows a man in Jewish garb,
briefcase in hand, walking down a busy city street. He's on
his cell phone telling someone, "And remember, if you need
anything, I'm available 24/6."

The idea of a day off doesn't mean that Shabbat is to be
marked by worldly amusement and leisure. "It is a day filled,
not with vain pursuits, but with edifying ones . . . a day
intended to refresh the soul."[17]

2. Sabbath is an exercise in **remembrance**.
Setting aside life's urgencies, observers of Shabbat are able
to recall all that is important. They remember with awe the

creation of the world—that all people and things belong to the one who made them. In ceasing their labors, they remember Egypt's oppressive taskmasters who made the Israelites labor endlessly—and feel gratitude for God's deliverance. Finally, they remember the eternal covenant that God made with Israel—the Sabbath serving as a perpetual sign of the Almighty's promise to make the Israelites a holy people (Exodus 31:13).

Through the hectic hubbub of the workweek, it's easy to forget these eternal realities and slip into a kind of spiritual slumber. Sabbath involves waking up to ultimate truths and being mindful. This does not mean, however, that the Sabbath is a somber and gloomy exercise.

3. Sabbath is a time for **rejoicing**.

At sunset on Friday in Jewish communities, the spirit of anticipation is tangible. The mood is festive. Dressed-up family members sit down to a candlelit feast. As the wine flows, the joy increases, often expressing itself through Sabbath songs. Funny stories are told. As Anita Diamant says, "*Shabbat* is not a solemn occasion. Along with the candles, wine, and *challah*, smiles and laughter belong at the table."[18]

4. Sabbath is a focus on **relationships**.

The goal of Shabbat—and all Jewish holidays—is intimacy with God and connection with the people of God. Rushing through life at a breakneck pace, most people offer up hurried, half-hearted prayers (if they think to pray at all). Or they are physically present but emotionally distracted in their interactions with loved ones, coworkers, and friends. On Shabbat, by stepping away from all the electronic gadgets that have conditioned us to jump every time they beep, the stresses of everyday life begin to dissipate. Celebrants create the time and space necessary to engage with God and one another on a deep and meaningful heart level.

5. Sabbath is an opportunity to **reorder** one's soul.

The cessation of everyday busyness brings moments of stillness. Here is an opportunity for solitude and study. The Talmud teaches that God gave Israel the Sabbath for this very reason, that his people might study the Torah. To paraphrase Norman Lamm, it is through quiet meditation that

Sabbath celebrants are able to make themselves available to higher impressions.[19] This kind of quiet reflection provides needed perspective. It recalibrates the heart and restores a sense of sanity to the soul.

6. Sabbath is an invitation to **renewal**.

Rabbi Irving Greenberg has said that Shabbat is not simply a day of being. It is also "a day of becoming."[20] Through the ages, the Jewish people have discovered that the twin practices of reading the sacred texts and praying together with God's "holy people" (Deuteronomy 28:9) have a transformative effect. In this regard, observing the Sabbath is a highly practical way of carrying out the mitzvah (i.e., commandment) of Leviticus 19:1–2: "The LORD spoke to Moses: 'Speak to the entire Israelite community and tell them: Be holy because I, the LORD your God, am holy'" (CSB).

After six days in a gritty world that continually chips away at our integrity and smudges our souls, the seventh day is a gracious invitation to enter into a purposeful time of renewal and re-creation.

7. Sabbath is a time of **recommitment**.

Greenberg further explains three important things that Shabbat does: (1) it gives us a tantalizing glimpse of the redeemed world yet to come; (2) it invites us to briefly savor that perfection; and (3) it commands, "Now, go and make it happen!"[21]

Through the "taste of paradise" that is Shabbat, the people of God are reenergized. They find new resolve. With joyful hearts and holy intention, they are equipped to go and "repair the world" (*tikkun olam*).

How significant is Shabbat to the Jewish people? Consider this: it is the only day of the week when funerals and weddings are prohibited. Indeed, all expressions of overt mourning are prohibited. Fast days that fall on Shabbat are moved to the following day—the only exception is Yom Kippur. And Shabbat is the only day of the week with a name. The other six days are described solely in terms of their relationship to the Sabbath: "the first day toward Shabbat," "the second day toward Shabbat," and so forth. Jews spend the week waiting, preparing for, and looking forward to Shabbat. A new item of clothing, a new serving dish, a new toy acquired during the week—all are saved to be enjoyed first on Shabbat.

The implication is clear: all aspects of Jewish life and time, including all the other holidays, revolve around Shabbat. It is the apex, the crown, of each week. It is holy and set apart from all other days. It is, in the words of Joseph of Hamadan, "a soul for the other six days; they derive their nourishment . . . from it."[22]

The Practices of Sabbath

Thinking of Shabbat in three parts—Friday night, Saturday morning, and Saturday afternoon—helps us understand the various aspects of observing Sabbath.

Just as Sunday worship customs vary from one Christian family or congregation to another, Shabbat traditions look different in different Jewish homes and synagogues. But one reality never changes: restrictions against engaging in creative labor *on* the Sabbath require a good bit of planning and preparation *before* the Sabbath.[23]

Much of this planning involves food preparation. (Remember: Shabbat is a day full of good food, and plenty of it!) But other responsibilities—work/business demands, laundry, shopping, errands, house cleaning, yard work—must also be handled in advance too. Still, there are always things left undone. And, spiritually speaking, this is the point. Shabbat is the time when no matter how incomplete the fruits of our labor are in this world, we are happy with and accepting of creation as it is. Even if the laundry didn't get folded, it's a reminder to be grateful for what is, and to wait patiently for what could and should be.

What Happens during the Friday Night Shabbat Celebration? The table is set on Friday with the best a family has: this might include fine linen, crystal, china, and silver, or a white tablecloth and special Shabbat dishes. As the sun begins to set, it is common in many Jewish homes for mothers or children to bring out small tin cans or containers.[24] These boxes are used to collect money for various charitable organizations. Anita Diamant describes this practice, called *tzedekah*, as "a way of both sharing happiness and of recalling that the world requires our attention."[25]

No later than eighteen minutes prior to sunset, the evocative Shabbat candle-lighting ceremony takes place. The
woman of the house lights at least two lights, usually in the
form of wax candles or oil with wicks. The candlesticks used
in this ceremony are typically beautiful, adhering to the
rabbinical principle of hiddur mitzvah. In the warmth and
glow of the candlelight, blessings are then spoken. The parents bless the children. The priestly blessing from Numbers
6:24–26 is pronounced. Some families sing the well-known
"Shalom Aleichem," a song acknowledging the presence
of God's angels on Shabbat. This is followed by one of the
most beautiful familial moments of the week: singing
aloud together from Proverbs 31 (vv. 10–31) before the
meal. This offers the family a chance to remember how
much of the planning, preparation, and atmosphere of
Shabbat is made possible by remarkable, hardworking
wives and mothers.

Next, the wine is consecrated in a ceremony called the
kiddush. Some families stand; others sit. Some drink from a
single cup or goblet; others, from separate glasses. In every
case, the vessels used are special and beautiful.

A hand-washing ritual follows, along with another prayer. Then comes the blessing over the bread (called challah). Easy to make, challah is a rich, sweet bread with a soft texture that is often shaped into a braid. Hearkening back to God's command to the ancient Israelites to collect a double portion of manna before the Sabbath (Exodus 16:22–23), it is customary to have two challah loaves on the table. These loaves are typically covered by attractive embroidered cloths.

 ## What's Kiddush?

The Torah commands God's people to "remember the sabbath day, and keep it holy" (Exodus 20:8). The verb translated "remember" is the Hebrew word *zachor.* Because this word is used in connection with wine elsewhere in the Bible (see Song of Solomon 1:4 and Hosea 14:7), Jews engage in a special kiddush ceremony (the word means "to make holy" or "to consecrate") at the beginning of Sabbath and on other holy days in which a standard prayer of blessing is said over the wine in Hebrew: *Barukh Atah Adonai, Eloheynu Melekh ha-olam, boray p'ree ha-gafen.* Translated, this means "Blessed are You, Eternal One our God, King of the Universe, Who creates the fruit of the vine."

Finally, the Shabbat Friday night meal officially begins. And what a feast! Food is so important, such an indispensable part of Jewish life, that Rabbi Eliezer wrote, "If there is no flour, there is no Torah."[26] Even families that are not financially prosperous strive to make the Friday night dinner memorable. The goal isn't so much to be fancy as it is to make the occasion special, to make a little more effort for things to stand out.

Many families sit around the table and engage in focused, unhurried conversation. This is also a time for guests, when there is abundant time to welcome friends and relatives

 What's a Kippah?

The Talmud says, "Cover your head, so that the fear of Heaven will be upon you" (Shabbat 156b). This explains why observant Jewish males (and these days, also some females) wear a *kippah*, a traditional round cap, brimless and typically embroidered or made of cloth. In Yiddish, it is called a yarmulke. This head covering is not a fashion statement. It's a way of showing humility before God and honor to God, a way of reminding the wearer to be reverent in thought, word, and deed.

together to join in the Sabbath joy. In more religious homes, the meal is eaten late, so that the family can attend services at the synagogue (*shul* or *beit knesset*), where congregants greet one another with the phrase *Shabbat Shalom* ("Sabbath peace be upon you").

After the meal (cleanup is usually kept to a minimum), as after all meals, Jews recite the *Birkat Ha'Mazon* prayer, the

 What's a Mezuzah?

Deuteronomy 6 contains the Shema, one of the most familiar and beloved passages in the Bible. In these verses, the people of God are commanded to love the one true God exclusively and wholeheartedly, to live out all his commands, and to pass on their faith to their children. In addition to binding his commandments on their hands and wearing them as emblems on their foreheads (v. 8), God further commands his people to "write them on the doorposts" of their houses and gates (v. 9).

The word translated "doorpost" in this passage is the Hebrew word *mezuzah*. For this reason observant Jews obtain verses of the Shema handwritten

"Grace after the Meal." On Shabbat, this prayer has some special additions. And in the spirit of unhurried joy that is Shabbat, the prayer is often sung together to happy melodies.

It is not surprising that with such an intense focus on drawing closer to God and others on Shabbat, Friday night for many Jewish couples culminates in physical intimacy. How's

by scribes on parchment (the skin of kosher animals). These parchments are then rolled up and inserted into metal cases or wooden boxes that hang on the doorposts or on the right-hand side of the doors in their homes (except for bathrooms). *Mezuzot* (the plural form of *mezuzah*) are hung at eye level, roughly a third of the way down from the lintel, usually at an angle, with the upper end pointed inward. A small opening in the box reveals on the back of the parchment the Hebrew word Shaddai, which means "Almighty."

These mezuzot, always visible as household members go about the day, serve as reminders of divine protection and also of human responsibility to live according to God's law.

that for a mitzvah! (And some people thought Shabbat was boring.)

What Happens on the Morning of Shabbat?

On Saturday mornings, many families make their way to the synagogue for a service featuring prayers, readings from the Torah and the Prophets, and usually a related sermon or discussion of the biblical text. A community kiddush service/lunch may follow at the synagogue. Some Jewish families choose to observe the morning by staying home and reading the Torah, and leading their children in Shabbat-themed songs and playing board games.

Lunch might consist of stew—simmering since Friday afternoon—sandwich trays, or casseroles prepared prior to Shabbat.

What Happens on Shabbat Afternoon?

After lunch, the day features spending time with loved ones, relaxing, playing board games, retelling family stories, napping. Some go on nature strolls. Some read. Others engage in Torah study with friends or check on elderly or shut-in neighbors. Before sunset, the final meal of Shabbat—the simplest but most spiritually significant of the day's three meals—is eaten.

The Sabbath ends, literally, when the heavens give the word (i.e., when three stars become visible in the night sky). This dusk-to-evening moment signals that it's time for the Havdalah ritual (the word means "distinction" or "separation"). A cup of wine is filled to overflowing to symbolize the hope for overflowing blessings in the week ahead. The Havdalah candle—made of two or more braided candles—is lit. The cup is lifted and blessed (but not drunk until the conclusion of Havdalah). Then, aromatic spices—a kind of spiritual smelling salts—are brought out and passed around. (As happens with other religious rituals, the Havdalah service appeals powerfully to the senses, especially the sense of smell.) Most families have a spice box, which they fill with cloves or other fragrant spices.[27] This ritual is intended to console the spirit upon its "loss" of the Sabbath. Of course, the delightful scents also serve to remind celebrants of the sweetness of the paradise that is Shabbat. The act of savoring these smells becomes a prayer for a sweet week to come. Many Jews admit that the Havdalah service at the end of Shabbat, though moving and beautiful, leaves them with a bittersweet feeling.

In her memoir about growing up Jewish in the early 1900s in Mukachevo, Czechoslovakia, Gabriella Auspitz Labson shares vivid and moving memories of Shabbat. She remembers the huge, live carp swimming each Friday in the family bathtub—the unwitting entrée of the evening feast. She still sees her father's hands above her head, hears him speaking a weekly blessing over her—that she might one day become as great as Sarah, the wife of the Jewish patriarch Abraham. She recalls all those mystical Havdalah ceremonies on Saturday evenings during which she would stand on a chair holding the lit twisted candle as high as she possibly could. (She had been told that the higher she stretched, the taller her future husband would be!)

Labson remembers the hot wax dripping down onto to her arm, and her father saying, "See . . . even the candle weeps when the Shabbat is leaving us." She recollects the pleasing aroma of the spice box, extinguishing the candle in the wine, singing two last songs, and wishing each other a good week. And the moment she disliked most? Turning the lights back on throughout the house when Shabbat was over.[28]

This is how we know something is sweet. We feel bittersweet when it is gone.

THE FESTIVALS

The Torah prescribes three pilgrimage festivals annually for the Jewish people—one after the spring harvest, another at the summer harvest, and a third at the time of the fall harvest. In ancient temple times, the Israelites were commanded to bring offerings to Jerusalem to celebrate these festivals. All Israelite men were obligated to do so *in person* and were allowed to make sacrifices on behalf of the women and children of their households.

In Exodus 23:14, God commands, "Three times in the year you shall hold a festival for me."

The three festivals specified by the Almighty are (1) "the festival of unleavened bread"; (2) "the festival of harvest, of the first fruits of your labor"; and (3) "the festival of ingathering at the end of the year, when you gather in from the field the fruit of your labor" (vv. 14–16). Today, these three festivals are more commonly known as Passover (or Pesach), Shavuot, and Sukkot.

Pesach (pronounced *PAY-sackh*) is the festival that takes place each spring (March/April). It's also known as Passover and the Feast of Unleavened Bread.

Shavuot (pronounced *shah-voo-OT*) takes place during early summer (May/June). You will sometimes hear it referred to as the Feast of Weeks or Pentecost.

Sukkot (pronounced *SUE-cot*) is a fall celebration (September/October) also called the Feast of Tabernacles or Festival of Booths.

The word *festival* tells us about the spirit of these holidays. They are *festive* occasions, marked by *feasting*. The goal? To celebrate with great joy in God's presence and to be generous with the blessings the Almighty has himself so generously supplied.

Passover

"The rituals associated with the Passover Haggadah allow us to reexperience slavery and freedom, incarceration, and liberation, so that we are liberated anew each year as much as in the era of Moses."

—Rabbi Shmuley Boteach

In the 1800s, Jews all over the world began trickling back to the land of their forefathers. This wide-scale, long-term relocation was fueled partly by anti-Semitism and partly by the universal human longing for home. But even in Zion (i.e., Jerusalem) and other cities rich in Jewish history, the freedom and peace sought by these Jewish returnees was elusive. Their swelling numbers created tension with the Arab residents of Palestine. In 1922, when the League of Nations proposed creating a permanent homeland for the Jews, the situation became violent.

In 1936, a Jewish leader named David Ben-Gurion spoke to the Peel Commission (formed by the British government to help develop a partition plan for lasting peace). Here is part of what he said:

> [Three hundred] years ago, there came to the New World a boat, and its name was the Mayflower. The Mayflower's landing on Plymouth Rock was one of the great historical events in the history of England and in the history of America. But I would like to ask any Englishman sitting here on the commission,

what day did the Mayflower leave port? What date was it? I'd like to ask the Americans: do they know what date the Mayflower left port in England? How many people were on the boat? Who were their leaders? What kind of food did they eat on the boat?

More than 3,300 years ago, long before the Mayflower, our people left Egypt, and every Jew in the world, wherever he is, knows what day they left. And he knows what food they ate. And we still eat that food every anniversary. And we know who our leader was. And we sit down and tell the story to our children and grandchildren in order to guarantee that it will never be forgotten. And we say our two slogans: "Now we may be enslaved, but next year, we'll be a free people."[29]

At a critical moment in Jewish history, notice how David Ben-Gurion hearkened back to what many consider the single most crucial moment in Jewish history.

The Origins of Passover

Passover is the holiday banquet that commemorates the end of great suffering. It is surely Judaism's most widely celebrated holiday. This Feast of Unleavened Bread is observed for seven days—eight for Jews outside Israel—beginning on Nissan 15 (the first month of the Jewish calendar). This means Pesach (as it is called by the Jewish people) routinely occurs during March or April on the Gregorian calendar. How fitting that a holiday commemorating Israel's redemption from slavery takes place in the springtime—a season of rebirth and hope—in the land promised to Abraham and his descendants.

Exodus 12 explains the original Passover celebration, but a bit of a backstory is helpful. Let's review the ancient story that has been retold around Jewish dinner tables all over the world every Passover for more than three millennia.

In the final chapters of Genesis we meet Joseph, the great-grandson of the Hebrew patriarch Abraham. Betrayed by his jealous brothers, this gifted young man ends up a lowly servant in Egypt. He suffers unjustly but eventually

rises to become Pharaoh's most trusted adviser. In that ca-
pacity, Joseph helps his "adopted nation" not merely survive
an extended famine but prosper through it. Joseph also
reunites with his family and moves them to Egypt, where he
can provide for them. There, the descendants of Abraham
become twelve flourishing tribes.

By the opening chapters of Exodus, however, the picture
isn't quite so rosy. Much time has passed. Egypt's new ruler
feels no obligation to honor Joseph's memory or favor his
family. On the contrary, he conscripts the Hebrew people
into his labor force. Then, alarmed at how fast their number
is growing, Pharaoh orders that all Hebrew newborn males
be thrown into the Nile River.

Moses is one of those condemned babies. Indeed, his
mother actually does put him in the Nile—but in a float-
ing basket. Mercifully, he is rescued—and adopted—by the
daughter of Pharaoh. For some forty years, Moses enjoys
all the privileges of Egyptian royalty. But one day he sees an
Egyptian overseer beating a Hebrew laborer. Moses saves
the victim by killing his attacker. Then, fearing for his safety,

he flees the country. In the desolate wilderness of Midian, the fugitive Moses begins building a new life.

Meanwhile, back in Egypt life grows even more unbearable for the captive Hebrews. At long last, God responds to their heartfelt cries. He sends the all-but-forgotten Moses back to Egypt to lead the Hebrew people to freedom after appearing to him in the burning bush (Exodus 3).

Again and again, Moses delivers God's command to Pharaoh: "Let my people go" (Exodus 5:1). But the heart of Egypt's ruler is as stony as a desert sphinx. God responds by sending a series of devastating plagues, each one meant to change Pharaoh's heart and mind. The obstinate king will not budge, even as his nation is decimated by these calamities.

On the night of the tenth and final plague—the killing of all the firstborn in the land—God offers the Hebrew people a way to evade this judgment. Each family is commanded to slaughter a lamb and then smear its blood over their door. God's promise to those who obey? "When I see the blood, I will *pass over* you, and no plague shall destroy you when I strike the land of Egypt" (Exodus 12:13, emphasis added). Interestingly, the Hebrew word *pasach* is the verb translated "pass over."

For the Egyptians, this is a night of bitter wailing: "There was not a house without someone dead" (Exodus 12:30). For the Hebrews, it is a night of deliverance. Pharaoh *finally* relents. He doesn't just *allow* Moses and the Israelites to leave; he commands them, "Rise up, go away . . . be gone" (vv. 31–32).

The Hebrews waste no time. They hastily scoop up all their belongings—even their yeast-free bread dough (Exodus 12:34)—and leave. And the Egyptian people are so relieved to see them go, they shower their former slaves with farewell gifts of silver and gold.

It would be a great story if it ended right there. But like all good thrillers, the story of the exodus of the Hebrew people from Egypt includes a final plot twist. If you've read the story in Exodus or seen a movie version of these events—either Cecil B. DeMille's classic *The Ten Command-*

ments starring Charlton Heston (Paramount Pictures, 1956) or the animated *The Prince of Egypt* (DreamWorks, 1998)— you know what happens next. Pharaoh, the consummate villain, changes his mind yet again. He marshals his troops and takes off after the departing Hebrews.

Moses and the people have barely made it to the Red Sea before Pharaoh and his chariots come thundering into view. Suddenly the Israelites seem to have just three options, all of them terrible: plunge into the water and drown, attempt to fight the world's most feared army and be slaughtered, or surrender and return to a life of crushing slavery.

All is lost, right? Wrong. Moses raises his staff. Immediately, a strong east wind begins to blow, creating an escape route *through* the sea! But that's not the only miracle. While the Hebrew people hurry east to freedom between two great walls of water, the pursuing Egyptians are restrained by a massive "pillar of fire and cloud" (Exodus 14:19–24).

As soon as the Hebrews are safe on the other side, God removes his supernatural barricade. The Egyptian troops and chariots charge down into the seabed, hell-bent on destroying their former slaves. Moses stretches out his hand a second time. When he does, the two walls of Red Sea water collapse upon the advancing Egyptians. The Hebrews, who are safe, sing a great song of victory and praise to God (Exodus 15).

The Mitzvah of Passover

This is the breathtaking story celebrated by Jews each year at Passover. And isn't it interesting that God had the ancient Israelites celebrate their first Festival of Freedom *before* they were physically free? In Exodus 12:14–27, we read:

> This day shall be a day of remembrance for you. You shall celebrate it as a festival to the Lord. . . . Seven days you shall eat unleavened bread; on the first day you shall remove leaven from your houses, for whoever eats leavened bread from the first day until the seventh day shall be cut off from Israel. On the first day you shall hold a solemn assembly, and on the seventh day a solemn

assembly; no work shall be done on those days; only what everyone must eat, that alone may be prepared by you. You shall observe the festival of unleavened bread, for on this very day I brought your companies out of the land of Egypt. . . . "You shall observe this rite as a perpetual ordinance for you and your children. When you come to the land that the LORD will give you, as he has promised, you shall keep this observance. And when your children ask you, 'What do you mean by this observance?' you shall say, 'It

 Judaism's Pilgrim Festivals

"Countless multitudes from countless cities come, some over land, others over sea, from east and west and north and south at every feast. They take the temple for their port as a general haven in safe refuge from the bustle and turmoil of life, and there they seek to find calm weather, and, released from the cares whose yoke has been heavy upon them from their earliest years, to enjoy a brief breathing-space in scenes of genial cheerfulness."[30]
—An eyewitness account by Philo of Alexandria, first-century Jewish philosopher

is the Passover sacrifice to the LORD, for he passed over the houses of the Israelites in Egypt, when he struck down the Egyptians but spared our houses.'"

The Purpose of Passover

Here we see the purpose—and power—of Passover. It is a day of remembrance (Exodus 12:14). At Pesach, the incredible account of the Hebrew exodus is told through story, symbol, and song. Like no other, this story raises questions (v. 26) and starts discussions that help younger generations of Jews connect with their rich history. No wonder the Passover

 The Four Questions

A central part of the Passover Seder is when the youngest child present asks, "How is this night different from all other nights?" This happens during the Maggid portion of the evening. The leader of the Seder answers each of the following questions:
1. Why is matzah eaten?
2. Why is maror (i.e., bitter herbs) eaten?
3. Why is food dipped twice in salty water?
4. Why do we eat reclining?

event is at the core of the Jewish psyche—it heralds "the beginning of nationhood, the continuous survival of a people, and the importance of freedom."[31]

However, the holiday isn't meant to be a dry review of ancient history. On the contrary, participants are encouraged to personalize the story—to enter into it and imagine themselves walking *with* the ancient Israelites. The goal is to experience everything they encountered and felt. As we read in the *Pesach Haggadah*: "In every generation, each person must see himself as if he personally was liberated from Egypt."[32]

 What's a Seder?

Seder is a Hebrew word that means "order." It's what Jews call the big ceremonial feast they share at Passover. A Seder includes readings and recitations, telling stories, and singing songs. It includes a time of Q & A, eating symbolic foods, and participating in other meaningful traditions. In Israel, the Seder occurs on the first night of Passover. Jews living outside Israel celebrate the Seder on the first two nights of Passover.

Though synagogues do hold Passover services for the community, Pesach is primarily celebrated in homes. The family-centered, ritual-filled, highly interactive Seder meal is the holiday's focal point. Thus, it's not a celebration one simply throws together at the last minute.

Preparation for Passover

There's a reason that Rabbi Ted Falcon has joked that Passover is the Jewish holiday "most likely to elicit a groan."[33] Like any Jewish holiday, Passover preparations include

 Beautiful Haggadot

Haggadot (the plural form of *Haggadah*) are varied in content and appearance. They can be purchased online. Sometimes they are homemade, the result of much cutting and pasting. Certain Haggadot serve an aesthetic purpose and include lavish illustrations. Others are more practical in nature, containing copious explanations, historical notes, and step-by-step instructions. Many families pass down these Passover scripts through the generations until they gain the status of "desirable heirloom."

elaborate meal planning. There's also the business of selecting and reviewing the Haggadah (literally, "a telling"). A Haggadah is like a script or a road map for how the elements of a Passover Seder will unfold. It shows the order of events and contains all the biblical texts, prayers, and blessings needed for the observance.

Food and haggadah preparations pale, however, compared to practicing the mitzvah to "remove leaven from . . . houses" (Exodus 12:15). This is easily the most time-consuming—and exhausting—pre-Passover activity.

Any grain—wheat, oats, barley, spelt, or rye—that has been mixed with water and allowed to rise (i.e., it wasn't baked within eighteen minutes) is considered forbidden (*hametz*). It is leavened. The yeast in it has been allowed to activate, and this makes it unfit for consumption—or even ownership—on Passover. Anything and everything with leaven—not just food products—must be destroyed, sold to a non-Jew, or given away. Some families simply dispose of everything that is not clearly labeled "Kosher for Passover."

In observant families, this "no leaven" command triggers the ultimate spring-cleaning project. Homes—especially kitchens and dining rooms, where food is stored, prepared, and served—get inspected and polished to a shine from top to bottom.

In a 2012 essay called "Cleaning for Passover, Missing My Bubbe,"[34] actress Mayim Bialik, of the hit TV show *The Big Bang Theory*, fondly remembers her maternal grandmother as being unequalled in the art of Passover cleaning. "Give that 5-foot-tall, 5-foot-wide Hungarian *balabusta*[35] a sponge in a kitchen and by nightfall, the sink would take on a luster unseen before her thick hands set to it."[36]

Removing leaven is hard work. It involves scrubbing sinks; sweeping cracks; discarding floor mats; mopping floors; steam-cleaning carpets; scrubbing counters; emptying drawers; wiping shelves; and cleaning out pantries, cabinets, refrigerators, and freezers. It also means pulling out of storage a set of special, hametz-free pots, dishes, and silverware that are used only at Passover.

Some have noted that all this rigorous cleaning serves a double purpose: it not only gets all the leaven out of a home but also gives participants a deeper appreciation for their Jewish ancestors who were subjected to slave labor.

When all the cleaning is complete, the family engages in a kind of "hametz hunt" (*Bedikat Chametz*) the night before Passover starts. This involves a family member intentionally

 What's the Harm in Hametz?

Many naturally ask, Why such a fuss over hametz? Philo of Alexandria, a Jewish-Greek theologian-philosopher (and contemporary of Jesus) suggested that hametz is a symbol of pride. It is leaven, after all, that causes bread dough to puff up. And remember the Passover story? It was pride that caused Pharaoh's heart to swell with such arrogance that he repeatedly rejected God's command to let the captive Hebrews go (Exodus 5:2). Thus at Passover the goal is to search not just our homes but also our hearts for any traces of pride. When we find such attitudes, we are to sweep them thoroughly from our souls.[37]

hiding a few leavened items (e.g., some small pieces of bread) around the house. Then, using a candle, the other family members conduct a careful search of the house.

 ## Holiday Reading

As cultures celebrate holidays, interesting customs develop over time. Many Americans, for example, drag pine trees into their homes each December and scarf down hot dogs on the Fourth of July. In Jewish culture, a long-standing tradition is to read certain books of the Bible in conjunction with certain holidays. For example, Jonah is read on Yom Kippur, Ecclesiastes on Sukkot, and Ruth on Shavuot. On Passover, it's the Song of Solomon.

Anyone who has perused the Song of Solomon knows that it's a racy read—at times quite explicit. So the natural question is, What does *this* have to do with Passover? The rabbis suggest that the lovers in the Song of Solomon are metaphors for God and Israel. In a real sense, they argue, God's rescue of the Hebrews from Egyptian slavery amounted to a proposal of marriage. Thus, it only makes sense on Passover to read the Bible's most passionate love song.

When they find the offending food items, they use a feather to sweep them into a spoon—and this hametz is then placed in a paper bag with the contaminated spoon and feather. *Bittul Chametz* is the ritual in which a homeowner recites a formula of nullification. This declares the leavened material worthless—and amounts to an official renunciation of ownership. *Bi'ur Chametz* is the final cleaning ritual in which any remaining leavened material is destroyed (usually by burning it outside the following morning).

The Practices of Passover

At Passover, as at other Jewish holidays, families (and synagogues) collect a special tzedekah—in this case called *Ma'ot chittim*, "money for wheat."

If you are ever privileged to attend a Passover Seder, you'll sit down to an elaborately decorated table. Different families follow different orders and traditions, but you'll almost certainly observe a Seder plate containing these foods, each full of symbolism:

- *Karpas*—A green vegetable (typically parsley or celery), karpas hints at the new season of spring.

Before it is eaten, it is dipped in salt water, which symbolizes the bitterness and tears of the Israelites who suffered in slavery.

- *Zeroah*—A shank bone (often chicken or turkey in the Passover celebrations of Ashkenazic Jews;[38] typically lamb at the Passover observances of Sephardic Jews[39]), zeroah is meant to call to mind the Passover lambs roasted in those "sacred family barbecues" of ancient times.

- *Beitzah*—A roasted egg, the common food of mourners, beitzah is a sad reminder to grieve the destruction of the temple.

- *Maror* and *chazeret*—Bitter herbs (often horseradish and romaine lettuce—but any bitter vegetables are allowed), these items recall the harsh life of the captive Israelites.

- *Charoset*—A sweet chutney-like paste made of fruit, wine, and nuts, charoset serves to represent the mortar that the Israelites had to mix during their years of Egyptian slavery (although it has a much better flavor than mortar!).

The Pesach meal also includes the following:

- *Matzah*—Three large pieces of unleavened bread (that's what matzah means) are kept on a separate plate and covered by a cloth.

- *Wine* (or grape juice)—Participants typically drink four small cups during a Seder. These four cups represent God's four promises in Exodus 6:6–7: "I will free you. . . . [I will] deliver you. . . . I will redeem you. . . . I will be your God." A fifth promise in verse 8, "I will bring you . . ." is represented by a fifth cup, which is called "Elijah's cup." This cup is filled but not drunk during the Seder.

In the soft candlelight of Passover, a Seder includes fifteen parts:

1. *Kadesh*—saying a prayer or blessing over the wine and drinking the first cup.

2. *Urkhatz*—washing one's hands in a ritualistic way, but without saying the usual blessing.

3. *Karpas*—eating a green vegetable dipped in salt water.

4. *Yakhatz*—breaking the middle matzah on the special matzah plate. The bigger half of this piece is called

the *afikomen*; it is hidden by the children and will be sought out and eaten at the end of the meal.

5. *Maggid*—telling, from the family Haggadah, the story of the Israelite exodus. This part of the evening is unhurried, with children being encouraged to ask questions. Songs are sung, and the second cup of wine is drunk. This part of the evening is why some call the Passover Seder "the talking-feast."[40]

6. *Rakhtzah*—washing of the hands again, in anticipation of the meal, but this time as participants say the blessing.

7. *Motzi*—raising and blessing the matzah.

8. *Matzah*—eating the matzah; the sages say that one should eat at least an olive-sized piece.[41]

9. *Maror*—consuming the bitter herbs, dipped first into the charoset.

10. *Korekh*—making and eating a little "Passover sandwich," as tradition says the Rabbi Hillel did in temple times. He put a bit of lamb and some bitter herbs between two pieces of matzah. Modern celebrants forego the meat, substituting charoset instead.

11. *Shulkhan Orekh*—at last, eating the actual festive holiday meal! This means delicious kosher-for-Passover foods like gefilte fish, brisket, matzah-ball soup and other delicacies.

12. *Tzafun*—eating the affikomen. Remember the matzah that was hidden earlier in the evening? The kids bring it back and everyone eats it. Some families give a prize to the child who finds it.

13. *Barekh*—saying the blessing or grace at the end of the meal over a third cup of wine. In some homes, the front door is opened to allow the Israelite prophet Elijah to come in.

14. *Hallel*—singing praise songs to God and drinking the fourth cup of wine.

15. *Nirtzah*—ending the Passover Seder with the phrase "next year in Jerusalem," a kind of prayerful expectation of the messianic redemption, when all the exiles will be gathered back in their ancestral homeland.

The Meaning of Passover

One of history's most moving Passover accounts comes from the Bergen-Belsen concentration camp during the Holocaust.

With Passover approaching, some seventy Jews signed a petition requesting a small amount of flour so that they could make their own matzah and celebrate the holiday in the camp.

The camp commander stared with contempt at the rabbi delivering the petition but agreed to forward the request to Berlin. Then while patting his revolver, he added, "We will act according to their instructions."

Days passed with no word. Regrets surfaced. Fears mounted. Just when the signers of the petition were convinced they had signed their own death warrants, two big SS troopers—with two very large dogs—showed up. They escorted the group's rabbi to the commandant's office. All the way there, he silently prayed the *Vidui*, the prayer of confession that is commonly recited by Jews facing death.

To the rabbi's shock the commandant gave him not a bullet but good news. Berlin had approved the prisoners' request!

Immediately the group of grateful Jews at Bergen-Belsen went to work building a makeshift oven and baking a small amount of matzah. When Passover arrived, a Seder was held in one of the barracks. The gathered celebrants had no roasted egg, no charoset, no traditional greens, no roasted shank bone. But they had their shapeless, blackened matzah—and, metaphorically speaking, an ample supply of bitter herbs.

As tears streamed down faces in the moonlight, the youngest child present asked the poignant question, "How is this night different from all other nights?" The old rabbi, filled with faith and hope, responded. He acknowledged that they were living in perhaps the darkest night in history. But then he quoted the prophet Isaiah: "The people who walk in darkness will see a great light; those who live in a dark land, the light will shine on them" (Isaiah 9:2, NASB).

He kissed each of the children on the forehead "and reassured them that the darkest night of mankind would be followed by the brightest of all days."[42] Some of them later said they could have sworn they heard echoes of the Jewish messiah's footsteps in their own as they made their way back to their barracks.

Shavuot

"If Passover is a liberation, the question remains, a liberation
toward what? Freedom does not lie in anarchy; rather it is
found at Sinai."

—Michael Strassfeld

A Jewish folktale says that when word got out that God was planning to deliver the Torah to Moses on a mountaintop in the ancient Near East, each of the mountains in the region began making a case for why it should be the site of such a momentous event.

The tallest mountain touted the obvious fact that it was closest to heaven. A majestic mountain trumpeted its breathtaking beauty. A craggy, remote peak bragged, "I am most worthy because of my inaccessibility." Only the smallest mountain, Sinai, said nothing.

At last God spoke to the mountains, "Stop your arguing. I will not be giving the Torah on the highest or most treacherous mountain or even the most glorious summit. I will meet Moses on the humblest and smallest mountain among you."

And so God chose Mount Sinai.

The Origin of Shavuot

We should clarify that the Bible says *nothing* about bickering mountains. However, it does say that Mount Sinai is where God gave Moses the Torah (Exodus 19:11).

Shavuot (the Hebrew word for "weeks") is the Jewish festival on which Jews celebrate this towering event. It's celebrated every Sivan 6 (which annually occurs in either May or June on the Gregorian calendar).

What's the history of Shavuot? In the Torah, Leviticus 23 and Deuteronomy 16 stipulate when Shavuot is to occur. From the time of Passover, God says, "You shall count off seven weeks. . . . You shall count until the day after the seventh sabbath, fifty days" (Leviticus 23:15–16). Here is why it is called Shavuot, the Feast of Weeks: it is separated from Passover by a "week" of weeks (i.e., seven weeks). This explains why it is also called Pentecost—it occurs fifty days after Passover.

These passages show Shavuot to be a harvest festival situated midway between Israel's two other pilgrimage festivals. But unlike Passover in the spring and Sukkot in the fall—both of which are eight-day celebrations—Shavuot is only a one-day summer event (two days

 What's Lag Ba'Omer?

The seven-week period between Passover and Shavuot is referred to as the period of Sefirat HaOmer, the counting of the Omer. This is because worshipers were commanded on the second day of Passover to bring an *omer* (i.e., a sheaf) of new barley to the Jerusalem temple as an offering (see Leviticus 23:15–16). After that, with great joy and anticipation, celebrants would daily "count the Omer," literally count off forty-nine days, and on the fiftieth day celebrate Shavuot, when two wheat-based loaves were offered at the temple.

Following the destruction of the temple in 70 CE, the time of counting the Omer ceased to be a season of rejoicing. Jews remembered with sorrow Bar-Kokhba, the leader of a failed revolt against the ruling Romans. Some thought he was the Jewish Messiah, but he was killed in 135 CE. They outside Israel). Cantor Matt Axelrod jokes, "Poor

Shavuot. Picture this important festival, sitting on the

therapy couch, explaining how during its entire life it

always felt overshadowed by its two famous siblings,

Passover and Sukkot."[43]

also mourned the ten Talmudic scholars who were suspected by the Romans of being the instigators behind this uprising and subsequently massacred.

Chief among these spiritual teachers was Rabbi Akiva, who had thousands of loyal followers. When many of the rabbi's disciples died from a plague that struck during the Omer—and when the plague, according to tradition, suddenly ended on *Lag Ba'Omer* (i.e., the thirty-third day of the Omer period, Iyar 18)[44]—the day became an annual celebration now marked by bonfires and dancing. Lag Ba'Omer is the one up-beat day in an otherwise somber seven-week period.

Because the esteemed Rabbi Shimon bar Yochai is also said to have died on Lag Ba'Omer, some Jews make a special pilgrimage to his grave in Galilee on that day. Others also celebrate on Iyar 18 because they believe this to be the day on which God first gave the Israelites manna during their travel from the Red Sea to Sinai.

Now, to the question on the minds of observant Bible readers: If the Torah describes Shavuot as an agricultural festival requiring worshipers to bring the firstfruits of the harvest to Jerusalem to offer at the temple, why is it celebrated as the day on which God gave Israel the Torah at Sinai?

Scholars agree that the focus of Shavuot shifted following the destruction of the temple in 70 CE. Rabbis of the Talmudic era (i.e., the first five centuries of the common era) pointed to Exodus 19:1–3, which says that "Moses went up to God" during Sivan (the third month of the Jewish calendar). Most believed that God gave the Torah on Sivan 6. Thus, the holiday celebrating the firstfruits of the summer harvest is also the day on which the Jewish people celebrate the astonishing gift of the Torah. And thus the holiday with so many names earned yet another title: *Z'man Matan Torateinu*, "the time of the giving of our Torah."

The Revelation of Shavuot

According to the Bible, God didn't just huddle with Moses on Sinai once. There were multiple meetings. Depending on how you interpret the Torah, there were at least two back-and-forth trips.

The first visit involved God telling Moses that he wanted the people of Israel to be his "special treasure" and that he wanted their exclusive devotion (Exodus 19:3–6). If that sounds vaguely like a marriage proposal, it's because it was.

Good thing that Sinai *wasn't* extremely high or remote— and also that the octogenarian Moses was, apparently, in excellent physical condition. He scrambled back down the mountain and relayed God's offer. The people of Israel enthusiastically said, "We accept!" (v. 8).

 What's a Yad?

You may notice the reader of the Sefer Torah (the Torah scroll used during synagogue services) using a long pointer to keep his or her place. Called a *yad* (the Hebrew word for "hand"), this object is typically made of silver or wood, and the tip resembles a hand with a pointing index finger. A yad is used because Jewish tradition forbids touching a Torah scroll with one's bare hands.

The Israelites spent the next two days getting ready for the big event (vv. 10–12). As promised, God showed up on the third day—making quite the entrance. The Torah says a thick cloud, complete with fire, descended from heaven and covered the top of Sinai. There was a violent earthquake that shook the entire mountain. There were lightning strikes and the "blast of a trumpet so loud that all the people who were in the camp trembled" (v. 16). Every time Moses spoke, God responded "in thunder" (v. 19).

Exodus 20 suggests that God began to speak directly to the Israelites. But by the time he finished the Ten Commandments, they could take no more. God's glory was too great, his holiness too awesome. They asked Moses if he might serve as God's spokesman instead (v. 19).

So Moses ascended the mountain again. What happened next is a mystery the rabbis have debated for ages. Did God dictate the Torah to Moses word for word? Exodus 24:4 *does* say that "Moses wrote down all the words of the LORD." But Exodus 31:18 says that God did some writing too—that he gave Moses "the two tablets of the covenant, tablets of stone, written with the finger of God."

This much is certain: Moses hardly had time to admire Israel's magnificent new tablets before the Almighty was alerting him to trouble in the valley below. At least some of the people, because of Moses' extended absence (Exodus 32:1–6), had reneged on their promise to be devoted to God alone. They were worshiping an idol of their own making—a golden calf!

Moses wasted no time. He first begged God to forgive the Israelites. Once he was assured of God's mercy, he grabbed the stone tablets and started down the mountain.

For classic movie lovers, this is one of the best scenes in Cecil B. DeMille's *The Ten Commandments*. Charlton Heston (as Moses) is standing on a rock ledge, his red robe flowing, the skies of Sinai glowing red behind him. From this perch, he hurls angry words of condemnation at the wayward people scattered about him. Then, for dramatic effect, he hurls God's stone tablets at the calf idol. There's a terrific explosion. The ground opens up and swallows most of the guilty.

Hollywood special effects and creative license aside, the Bible *does* say that Moses angrily shattered the stone tablets (Exodus 32:19)—thereby prompting the observation that Moses is perhaps the only person in history to break all Ten Commandments at once. Afterward, he burned the calf idol and pulverized it into dust. Then he scattered all that ashy gold powder into a nearby stream and made the Israelites drink it. All these dramatic gestures were meant to symbolize how the Israelites had broken faith by breaking their covenant agreement with God.

Then it was back up the shrouded mountain for Moses. For the next forty days and forty nights the leader of the Hebrews and the God of the Hebrews were alone, and the future of the Hebrews seemed to hang in the balance. But when Moses finally showed up back in camp, he had a new set of tablets and a face that radiated with the glory of God (Exodus 34:29). Here was glorious proof that, despite their sin, God was still committed to the people of Israel.

The Practices of Shavuot

So what exactly do observant Jews do on this holiday that "commemorates the defining moment in all of Jewish history: the giving of the Torah, on Mount Sinai"?[45]

If you guess the festivities include a big meal, you're right, of course. At the Shavuot meal, dairy foods are front and center. In most homes, this means plenty of cheesecake

 Also on Shavuot . . .

In addition to God giving his law to Moses on Shavuot, other interesting claims are made about this day.

Some Jewish teachers say that it was on this day that the infant Moses was rescued from the Nile by the daughter of Pharaoh. Others assert that Israel's King David was born—and also died—on Shavuot. Israel ben Eliezer—better known as Ba'al Shem Tov—the renowned eighteenth-century Ukrainian rabbi, regarded as the founder of Hasidic Judaism, died on Shavuot in 1760.

and cheese blintzes. And while many explanations are given for this practice, perhaps the most common is that just as milk nourishes and sustains us physically (as infants), so too the Torah nourishes and sustains us spiritually.

Decorations typically include lots of greenery and flowers. Why? Perhaps because of Exodus 34:3. That's where God tells the Israelites not to let their flocks and herds graze in front of Sinai. Such a mitzvah would seem to imply an abundance of green grass.

The main activity at Shavuot, however, isn't eating cheese-cake or admiring the flowers. Observant Jews see the command to "be ready" to encounter God (Exodus 19:10–11) as a mitzvah to prepare their hearts. Some take a ritual bath (called a *mikvah*) in order to purify themselves for the reception of the Torah. But, bath or not, the core of Shavuot is expressed by staying up deep into the night reading, studying, and discussing the Jewish scriptures. Remember pulling all-nighters in college or grad school, and being so groggy the next day that you couldn't see straight? Shavuot is like that for many—but with much better study material.

One father and mother were talking about the Ten Commandments with their three children—ages eleven, eight, and six. After discussing the meaning of the fifth commandment, "Honor your father and your mother," the father paused and said, "Okay then, so God commands us to obey our parents when we are young and to respect our parents when we are old. Is there a commandment that tells us how to treat our brothers and sisters?" Without missing a beat, the oldest child glanced at his younger siblings and replied, "You shall not murder?"

All these assorted efforts at Bible study on Shavuot are forms of a practice called Tikkun Leil Shavuot, which means "the repairing night of Shavuot." There are many explanations for this custom. By giving undivided attention to the Torah, participants are acknowledging that in the past they have perhaps been lazy or slow in welcoming and doing

 The Torah Says That?

Most Jewish families at Shavuot, even if they don't forego sleep, do spend time discussing the Torah. This can lead to some interesting exchanges.

God's will. Some sources say that this practice is meant to rectify the Israelite people's sleeping in late on the day they were to receive the Torah, as one Jewish legend (*midrash*) has it.[46] However, on this day, by wakefully poring over the Jewish scriptures, Jews show their eager willingness to receive and study what they believe is God's word.

In synagogue services on Shavuot, congregations read Exodus 19–20, the stirring account of the giving of the Ten Commandments. It's customary also to read the book of Ruth. If you have forgotten that story, it's about a young, newly widowed Moabite woman who moves to Israel with her Hebrew mother-in-law. There she ends up remarrying, to an older Hebrew gentleman named Boaz, eventually becoming the great-grandmother of the great King David.

If this seems like an odd reading choice for a wheat festival that also commemorates the giving of the Torah, rabbis remind us of two facts. One, the book of Ruth takes place at harvest time. Two, Ruth's wholehearted embrace of the Hebraic faith symbolizes the way we should accept the teachings of the Torah, in loyalty and faithfulness.

The Meaning of Shavuot

In the same way that Passover encourages Jews to experience the incredible freedom that was given in the exodus from Egypt, Shavuot challenges Jews to experience the astonishing revelation given by God at Sinai.

Shavuot commemorates the "encounter of a whole people with the Holy."[47] Its purpose isn't merely to recall the giving

 The Broken Pieces

Some ancient Jewish sages claimed that the ark of the covenant—the gold-covered box that housed the second set of tablets God gave Moses on Sinai—also contained the pieces of the first set that Moses shattered after the people sinned so grievously.

If that's true, and not all rabbis believe it is, it prompts the question: Why keep such a grim reminder of sin? Because, some rabbis say, there are always lessons to be learned from the past, even from—and perhaps *especially* from—our failures. The broken tablets not only say something about human nature; next to the second set, they say something even more powerful about God's merciful character.

of the Torah in history. It's deeper and more personal: its purpose is to study the Torah and renew one's commitment to the way of Judaism. Torah study is not, as one man put it, "a point system for collecting merit badges from the Great Scoutmaster in the sky."[48] The purpose is to become a kingdom of priests and a holy nation. Author-journalist Abigail Pogrebin argues that Shavuot participants should be asking, "What am I supposed to do with my life?" She writes, "There's a 'supposed to' for each of us; we just need to discover it. We're not bestowed with life solely to exist, but to act."[49]

And the deep hope that sustains all those drowsy Torahstudiers in the wee hours of Shavuot? "Amid the thunder and lightning, the blaring of horns and dense smoke of our lives, the Voice can still be heard calling to us."[50]

Sukkot

"Sukkot is the time to learn the skill of happiness."
—*Rabbi Eliyahu Heller*

Ask Jane Kaufman, a newspaper editor in Springfield, Massachusetts, about her earliest, most memorable Jewish holiday celebration. She'll tell you about being four and finding herself gathered with family and friends under a neighbor's grape arbor. In fact, she still has a picture of the occasion.

Kaufman admits she had no idea at the time what the holiday was about, only that she "was intrigued at eating outdoors in the autumn under a darkening sky." She recalls being allowed to stay up much later than usual. "I liked the mystery," she remembers.

Only later did Kaufman come to understand the spiritual significance of this annual fall festival. Writing in a September 2013 article, she says it "may be the only Jewish holiday that has a prayer associated with sitting" in an outdoor "temporary booth."[51]

What is this "special and intimate" holiday that Kaufman further describes as being "about trusting the elements" and "hospitality"?

Sukkot.

To understand this little-known Jewish holiday, let's start with the Gentile holiday of Thanksgiving. Did you know that the Pilgrims likely ate duck, not turkey, at their famous 1621 feast? Did you further know that those "original" Plymouth Rock thanks-givers were actually emulating a much older biblical holiday? It's true: Miles Standish and friends modeled their big, invite-the-neighbors-over fall feast after the Jewish festival known as Sukkot. (This is actually a handy trivia fact to toss into the conversation this coming November when gathered family members start bickering over cranberry sauce and politics.)

Sukkot is, for all practical purposes, the "Jewish Thanksgiving."[52] Since the time of Moses, at the beginning of the annual fall harvest, the people of Israel have celebrated this week-long festival (from the 15th to the 21st of the Jewish month of Tishrei). It is variously known as the Festival of Booths, the Feast of Tabernacles, the Holiday of Ingathering, and *Zeman Simchateinu* (which means "Season of our Joy").

In Bible times, Sukkot was one of Judaism's three "pilgrimage festivals" (the other two being Passover and Shavuot). Together, these major holidays recall the earliest years and greatest events of Jewish history. Passover celebrates God's rescue of the Hebrews from slavery in Egypt. Shavuot commemorates God's giving of the Torah to the children of Israel at Mount Sinai. Sukkot remembers God's protection and provision for Israel during its years of wilderness wandering after leaving Sinai. It's no wonder that, until the destruction of the temple in 70 CE, every year—on each of these holidays—tens of thousands of Israelites made their way to Jerusalem to celebrate.

Sukkot derives its name from the Hebrew word that means "booth" or "hut." A *sukkah* (the plural is *sukkot*) is a temporary dwelling, similar to the kind of makeshift shelters the Israelites lived in during their decades of wandering and during each year's fall harvest.

> *"Passover celebrates a moment of pure triumph. Sukkot celebrates a seemingly endless forty-year journey. Passover is the holiday of faith; Sukkot is the holiday of faithfulness."* [53]
> **—Rabbi Irving Greenberg**

Only five days after the High Holy Days (Rosh Hashanah and Yom Kippur) that heavily encourage quiet and somber reflection, the Jewish people have to switch gears quickly. Suddenly, it's time for exuberant rejoicing! It's time to thank God for the harvest.

The Origin of Sukkot

Sukkot wasn't a human idea. According to the Torah, God commands its observance. The first mention of this annual harvest holiday is in Exodus 23:16: "You shall observe the festival of harvest, of the first fruits of your labor, of what you sow in the field. You shall observe the festival of ingathering at the end of the year, when you gather in from the field the fruit of your labor."

In Leviticus, we get more details, including the command to live in booths (i.e., sukkot):

> Now, the fifteenth day of the seventh month, when you have gathered in the produce of the land, you shall keep the festival of the LORD, lasting seven days; a complete rest on the first day, and a complete rest

on the eighth day. On the first day you shall take the fruit of majestic trees, branches of palm trees, boughs of leafy trees, and willows of the brook; and you shall rejoice before the LORD your God for seven days. You shall keep it as a festival to the LORD seven days in the year; you shall keep it in the seventh month as a statute forever throughout your generations. You shall live in booths for seven days; all that are citizens in Israel shall live in booths, so that your generations may know that I made the people of Israel live in booths when I brought them out of the land of Egypt: I am the LORD your God. (Leviticus 23:39–43)

In Deuteronomy, we see the command (an echo from Leviticus) that Sukkot is to be a time of extreme gladness: "Rejoice during your festival, you and your sons and your daughters, your male and female slaves, as well as the Levites, the strangers, the orphans, and the widows resident in your towns. Seven days you shall keep the festival to the LORD your God at the place that the LORD will choose; for the LORD your God will bless you in all your produce and in all your undertakings, and you shall surely celebrate" (16:14–15).

This point is not to be missed. Sukkot is a holiday of un-
bridled joy. Strassfeld writes, "Whether this is because we
have successfully completed the harvest or because we have
finished the process of repentance in the Days of Awe, we
are meant to have a sense of fulfillment and security."[54]

Sukkot is celebrated with gladness for two additional reasons: One, Solomon dedicated Israel's first temple on the
occasion of this feast (1 Kings 8:1–2). Two, looking ahead
to the future reign of the expected messiah, many believe
that it will be on Sukkot that all the nations will stream to
Jerusalem (Zechariah 14:16).

The Practices of Sukkot
Obviously you can't very well celebrate a Festival of Booths
if you don't have a booth. Thus, the building of a sukkah is a
primary preparatory step in celebrating Sukkot.

The question of what constitutes a proper sukkah has been
the subject of endless debate. Rabbinical teaching says that
a sukkah must have at least two and a half walls (i.e., it can
simply lean up against an existing structure). The issue of

walls *aside* (pun intended), all agree that it's the roof that is the most critical part of the structure.

The top of a sukkah is to be made out of something called *s'chach* (this refers to anything grown from the ground and then cut or chopped—for example, palm fronds, tree branches, cornstalks, bamboo shoots). These boughs and limbs need to be leafy enough to provide some shade but sparse enough to (a) enable those inside the sukkah to see the stars at night and (b) *not* be completely waterproof. (Apparently a little rain never hurt anybody—and actually, many of the prayers prayed during Sukkot are appeals to the Almighty *for* rain so that the harvest might be abundant.) Indeed, in the land of Israel it is precisely at this time that the first gentle rains begin to fall.

The mitzvah requiring families to "live in" this ramshackle shelter (Leviticus 23:42) for an entire week gets interpreted in all sorts of creative ways. Some consider this command fulfilled by eating a single meal in one's hut (or even in a friend's sukkah), or by sitting briefly in the sukkah for a short time each day during the festival. Many eat all their meals for the week in the sukkah and even sleep there. Through the centuries, noted rabbis have acknowledged the exemption from this command in the case of extreme discomfort or inclement weather. "In this way, they try to ensure that the *sukkah* will be seen as a symbol of joy, not as a burden."[55]

In observing this week of happy camping (or quick picnicking), some families prefer not to start from scratch. These busy, non-builder types opt for prefabricated sukkah kits, available online or in stores. Sukkot are usually decorated inside—with children's art, images of the land of Israel, or pictures of great rabbis. There is at least a table and chairs inside for people to eat, and lighting of some kind. No matter what an individual sukkah might look like, Cantor Matt Axelrod explains, "It's the opposite of the story of the three little pigs—the least durable and most vulnerable structure is what you're going for."[56] Or as Isidor Margolis observes, a rickety hut is preferable: "When we sit in a Sukkah, we express our faith in and reliance on God."[57]

If you ever get the opportunity to be in Israel at Sukkot, you'll see booths everywhere: army bases and public spaces, parks and parking lots. Some have likened the spectacle to a giant tailgate party before a major sporting event in America—the difference being, this ancient Jewish custom is *national* and it goes on for more than a week! The thought of celebrating Sukkot raises myriad questions: What if it's hot outside? Or cool? What about bugs? How does this work for those living in a big city? What might the neighbors think?

One story, perhaps apocryphal, is told of a devout Jewish family that moved into a posh high-rise in New York City. Just before Sukkot, the family erected a sukkah on their balcony and made plans to live in it for the following week. Almost immediately, several of their wealthy, non-Jewish neighbors filed a restraining order, claiming that the hut was an eyesore and violated numerous city codes (not to mention their high-society sensibilities).

The next day, the two sides were in court, standing before a judge who happened to be Jewish. After hearing from both parties, the judge began lecturing the builder of the sukkah: "You don't live in some low-rent neighborhood! You can't

just build a makeshift hut on Park Avenue! What's more,
you can't build *anything anywhere* without a building per-
mit." Then with just the hint of a smile, the judge looked at
the defendant and said, "I hereby give you *eight days* to take
that hut down, or pay a thousand-dollar fine. Next case!"

In addition to building one's hut, the other necessary Sukkot
preparation involves acquiring "the fruit of majestic trees,
branches of palm trees, boughs of leafy trees, and willows of
the brook" (Leviticus 23:40). The fruit traditionally understood to fulfill this commandment is the rare, beautiful,
very costly citrus fruit known as the *etrog* or citron. In keeping with the tradition of hiddur mitzvah (i.e., the practice
of "beautifying the commandment"), families often search
long and hard, and spare no expense (sometimes paying as
much as $100 each), in locating the most exquisite *etrogim*
(plural) they can find, one per person. Each worshiper
also combines one palm frond (*lulav*), two willow boughs
(*aravot*), and three myrtle sprigs (*haddasim*) to make a kind
of "bouquet of branches." For simplicity's sake, many refer
to this entire bundle—and not just the palm frond—as the
lulav.

As commanded in the Torah, the first day of Sukkot is a *yom tov* (i.e., a day on which work is forbidden). According to the Mishnah (*Sukkah* 51 a–b), during the time of the temple, a special ceremony called "the Drawing of the Water" was performed at the end of that first day. This ritual is thought to be inspired by Isaiah 12:3, which says, "With joy you will draw water from the wells of salvation." The Jewish sages said that anyone who had never witnessed this joyful celebration "never saw celebration in his life."[58] In addition to pouring out water libations, participants in ancient times would sing, blow shofars, and dance around golden menorahs whose wicks were made of the priests' worn-out garments.[59]

On the first night of Sukkot, celebrants light candles in their sukkah while reciting prayers and blessings. Some engage in *ushpizin*, a ritual in which families symbolically invite honorary guests to join them in the sukkah. This guest list reads like a "who's who" of patriarchs (and, some would add, matriarchs) from Jewish history: Abraham, Isaac, Jacob, Joseph, Moses, Aaron, David. One for each night.

At services the next morning, the four plant species are taken up by worshipers (the palm, myrtle, and willow branch bouquet in one hand, the citron in the other). While reciting the *berakhah* (i.e., blessing), participants shake or wave these symbols of agricultural prosperity up and down and to the north, south, east, and west. Why? Strassfeld explains, "As we shake the *lulav* and *etrog* in

 The Rare and Beautiful Etrog

In late 1980, Yisroel Weisberger, an Orthodox Jew and seller of Judaica in New York, picked up the phone and called John Kirkpatrick, a Presbyterian California citrus farmer. The two men had never met, but as an importer of expensive etrogim (or citrons) from Israel, Weisberger was wondering if it might be possible to grow the fruit commercially in the United States. At that time, no one was doing so—probably because etrog farming is quite tricky. Infestations from the dreaded red citrus mite are common. Also, the finicky trees require a precise amount of sunlight. Even then, *if* the trees bear fruit, only perfect specimens are acceptable to Jewish customers who need unblemished fruit for their once-a-year Sukkot celebrations.

the six directions, we acknowledge God's surrounding presence."[60]

As with all Jewish holidays, *tzedakah* (gifts to charity) are made in connection with Sukkot. Hospitality is also a dominant feature of this weeklong festival. Many welcome others into their sukkah, or they visit other families and

At the end of an hour-long conversation, Kirkpatrick decided to give etrog farming a try. He even agreed to adhere to strict rabbinical standards. Soon the longtime citrus grower had imported from Israel—and planted on his farm—more than two hundred etrog trees.

As of 2018, the Kirkpatrick etrog farm (called Lindcove Ranch) is still in business, now run by John's son, Greg. With four acres devoted to producing kosher etrogs, the family is the leading grower of the prized fruit in the United States. Most of their etrogim are sold to suppliers on the East Coast. To show you how careful observant Jews are in the selection of an etrog, in 2010 only one out of every four etrogim from the Kilpatrick's farm—or about three thousand in all—was deemed acceptable for use in Sukkot celebrations.

sukkot around the neighborhood. There is also much music, dancing, and reading from the book of Ecclesiastes—which many find curious, since Ecclesiastes isn't exactly the happiest, most upbeat of Bible books. There are several explanations for this. One is that Ecclesiastes helps remind us that our happiness at this season should be focused not on the pursuit of empty worldly pleasure but rather on spiritual joy.

The Meaning of Sukkot

For those who actually sleep in their sukkah, the act of looking up through those dead branches into the vastness of the night sky provides some powerful symbolism. It's a stirring reminder that their lives are ultimately in the hands of the living God.

Rabbi Shmuley Boteach notes that many Jews emerge from the High Holy Days feeling spiritually insecure, imagining that perhaps God loves them only when they do righteous things. Thus, he says, "the Almighty provides a festival in which he hugs us, as it were, to show unconditional love and total acceptance. . . . Like two lovers who ecstatically celebrate their reunion after geographic or emotional dislocation, we rejoice with God and are heartened by his embrace."[61]

The climax of Sukkot's week of rejoicing is an eighth day of assembly commanded by the Torah (Leviticus 23:36). We turn our attention now to that holiday, Shemini Atzeret/ Simchat Torah, or what Cantor Matt Axelrod calls "the holiday that no one knows."[62]

Shemini Atzeret/Simchat Torah

"On Simchat Torah, . . . the Torah, too, wants to dance, so we become the Torah's dancing feet."

—Hasidic saying

A. J. Jacobs is a journalist who describes himself as Jewish—"in the same way the Olive Garden is an Italian restaurant"—and agnostic. From September 2005 through August 2006, Jacobs attempted to follow all the commands in the Bible, from being fruitful and multiplying to stoning sinners (albeit very discretely and with very tiny pebbles). He chronicled his funny, fascinating experience in *The Year of*

Living Biblically, which became a *New York Times* best seller. Fairly early on in his experiment, Jacobs found himself in Brooklyn, New York. The occasion? Celebrating Simchat Torah with a group of Hasidic Jews.

Jacobs could hardly believe what he witnessed on that October night: a sea of heavy-drinking, hard-dancing Jewish men, bouncing off each other in their black hats. He describes the noise as deafening. He writes, "I tell you, I've never seen such pure joy. It is thick, atmospheric, like someone had released a huge canister of nitrous oxide into the room."

On that strange night, Jacobs admits moments of panic— the fear that he might be trampled, literally, by the celebrating hordes. But he also experienced a strange happiness. "I don't know if I feel God. . . . But a couple of times that night, I feel something transcendent."[63]

The Origin of Shemini Atzeret/Simchat Torah

On the heels of the divine command to observe Sukkot, the seven-day festival of living in homemade huts (Leviticus

23:34), God tells Moses to tell the Israelites, "On the eighth day you shall observe a holy convocation . . . *it is a solemn assembly*" (v. 36, emphasis added; see also Numbers 29:35). In Hebrew the phrase "eighth day of assembly" is Shemini Atzeret.

Hebrew scholars note how the word translated "assembly"—*atzeret*—is closely related to the verb that means "to stop" or "to hold back." Because of this, some rabbis have suggested that in this command to stick around an additional day after Sukkot, God is saying, "Remain with me another day."[64] Imagine a heartsick parent in the driveway pleading with his or her children and grandchildren, "Don't go yet! Please, can't you stay one more night?"

Some people view this added-on eighth day, Shemini Atzeret, as an extension of Sukkot. It's not. It's technically a separate holiday. However, the Jewish sages' problem with treating Shemini Atzeret as a separate celebration was that it was a "blank" holiday. It didn't have a specific theme. Their solution was to conclude the yearly cycle of reading the Torah on this day. The theme of sticking around for one extra day after Sukkot to take joy in the Torah (i.e., Simchat Torah) thus gave Shemini Atzeret its distinct identity.

So why do Jews living outside Israel celebrate for two days? Remember how in ancient times it fell to the Jewish ruling council to officially announce each new moon (i.e., the beginning of each new month)? And remember how it took time to get that word to Jews living in remote areas? And remember how this problem was remedied by adding an extra day to holiday celebrations to prevent anyone from celebrating a holiday early or late? This is why and how (by early medieval times) Shemini Atzeret became a two-day affair outside Israel, with the *content* of the holiday (great joy in the Torah—Simchat Torah) being expressed in full on that second day.

Think of how taxing the American Thanksgiving holiday break is—those five days from Wednesday to Sunday. Now consider *nine* straight days, beginning with Sukkot on Tishrei 15 and going through the end of Simchat Torah on Tishrei 23. That's a *lot* of celebrating!

The Practices of Shemini Atzeret/Simchat Torah

What activities take place on these two days?

On Shemini Atzeret, the Torah forbids all work. Synagogue services are held instead. Worshipers recite a prayer for rain called Tefillat ha-Geshem (the idea is "Okay, God, now that we're done living in a sukkah, let the skies open up"). Then an additional service (called a *Musaf* service) is held, and it includes more prayers for rain.

The seriousness of the occasion is shown by several factors: the rabbi and/or cantor dons his *kittel* (the same white robe worn on Judaism's holiest day, Yom Kippur); the prayer for rain is set to special music. This tune is reminiscent of melodies used during dramatic moments in the Passover and Yom Kippur observances. Finally, at the conclusion of the Shemini Atzeret midday service, communities engage in the recital of Yizkor, a memorial prayer service for the dead.[65]

All this sounds somber—nothing like A. J. Jacobs' wild, emotional experience. Where's all that Simchat Torah (i.e., "rejoicing with the Torah") joy? Buckle up and hold on. Just wait and watch what happens when the synagogue community completes its annual public cycle of Torah reading and immediately begins the cycle again.

In the evening service, the Torah scrolls are removed from the ark (i.e., the holy storage cabinet that houses a synagogue's scrolls). Worshipers then engage in the ancient practice of *hakkafot* ("circlings")—that is, leaders first make circles around the interior of the synagogue while carrying the Torah scrolls and reciting prayers; then the congregation responds. As the scrolls pass, observers symbolically kiss the scrolls.

 What Happens to Old Torah Scrolls?

Suppose a synagogue's Sefer Torah is damaged during an overly exuberant Simchat Torah celebration. Or suppose it (or even a synagogue prayer book) simply becomes worn out from years of use. What then? What becomes of these sacred writings?

Because Torah scrolls and other texts used in synagogue worship contain the four-letter name of God (the Tetragrammaton), they are never destroyed. Commonly, they (together with old *mezuzot*

They do this by touching a passing Torah with a prayer book or prayer shawl and then bringing that item to their lips.

After completing a circuit around the synagogue with enthusiastic singing and energetic dancing, this process is repeated six additional times. Other synagogue members are given the opportunity to carry a Torah scroll and dance. As you might imagine, this celebration often goes deep into the night.

The repeated circling symbolizes the truth that there is no end to reading and carrying out the Torah. It's an echo of the words

and *tefillin*) are collected and stored in something called a *genizah* (a Hebrew word meaning "hiding place"). A genizah is a special room—often an attic or basement—at a synagogue or a storage facility adjacent the synagogue. This is a temporary storage place for such holy writings en route to a cemetery burial.

The world's most famous genizah was discovered at the Ezra Synagogue in Fustat (i.e., Old Cairo), Egypt, in 1896. A treasure trove of medieval Jewish documents, much of this collection can now be seen at the Cambridge University Library.

of Ben Bag-Bag, a first-century rabbi and disciple of Hillel: "Turn the Torah over and over for everything is in it. Look into it, grow old and worn over it, and never move away from it."[66]

The morning service of Simchat Torah includes the ark being opened again and the scrolls being carried around the room seven additional times with dancing (hakkafot). But in contrast to the service the night before, the hakkafot are followed by each and every synagogue member being called upon to read portions of the Torah aloud. These Torah readings are called *aliyot*.

In some synagogues, even children are given aliyot (this is the only time of the year when children who are not yet of bar or bat mitzvah age are allowed to read). The highlight of the service occurs when the final verses of the Torah (i.e., Deuteronomy 34) are read. This particular *aliyah* is usually given to an honored member of the congregation (referred to on this occasion as "the bridegroom/bride of the Torah").

Immediately following this reading (which completes the annual synagogue reading of the Torah cycle), the congregation exclaims, *"Chazak, chazak, venit chazek!"* (Translation: "Be strong, be strong, and let us summon new strength.") Then another respected member of the synagogue is privileged to read Genesis 1:1–2:3 from a second Torah scroll, beginning the cycle again. The Torah has no end.

The Meaning of Shemini Atzeret/Simchat Torah

Simchat Torah is technically not a holiday. It is rather a spirit of deep gladness in the Torah that gets expressed on the second day of Shemini Atzeret. This is the occasion on which Jews express their unabashed love for and joy in the Torah through unrestrained singing and dancing. Anyone who's ever been to a Simchat Torah celebration will tell you that dancing skills are *not* required. In these moments, exuberance matters far more than elegance and competence. Because of the spiritual ecstasy involved (and surely also because of the candy given out), many Jewish children say that Simchat Torah is their favorite of all Jewish observances.

Non-Jewish visitors are understandably stunned by this display of passionate spiritual revelry in the Torah. The English diarist Samuel Pepys reportedly visited a London synagogue in October 1663, unaware that it was Simchat Torah. He then watched in shock "as grey-bearded men holding Torah scrolls pranced and cavorted about the synagogue like young goats."[67] He perhaps wouldn't have been so surprised had he remembered how King David danced wildly before the ark in 2 Samuel 6:16.

Rabbi Dovid Rosenfeld explains, however, that dancing with a Torah scroll on Simchat Torah isn't a matter of spiritual posturing. The ritual signifies a person's close, personal connection to God and his commandments: "This is not only the Torah of the nation of Israel; it is my own Torah. And each of us holds the Torah and celebrates just what God's wisdom means to him personally. For everyone has his or her own . . . story, how the Torah has touched his life."[68]

Cantor David Axelrod says that "Shemini Atzeret and Simchat Torah are like twin siblings that look nothing alike. . . . Shemini Atzeret itself is really the culmination of Sukkot, with many of the same themes. . . . Simchat Torah is the exclamation point at the end of the entire High Holiday season."[69]

And yet these different observances make for a perfect pairing. On Shemini Atzeret, the focus is on a God who supplies life-giving rain. The following day, which is sometimes referred to separately as Simchat Torah, the focus is on a God who speaks life-giving words. After the quiet contemplation, the loud celebration. After a day of expressing dependence, a day of sheer delight.

THE HIGH
HOLY DAYS

Jews believe these holidays are much more than just dates on a calendar. They see in them a vivid picture of God's faithful love for his people. Are they right? Do the festivals and observances—upon closer inspection—really have a deeper, allegorical meaning?

The month of Elul, leading up to the official Jewish High Holy Days, is intended to be a time of reflection and spiritual preparation. Isn't this, some ask, analogous to a time of courtship?

Then comes Rosh Hashanah (pronounced *RAH-sha-sha-nuh* or *rosh-ha-sha-NAH*). The Jewish New Year is a time of serious commitment. Could this be intended to call to mind a betrothal?

Yom Kippur (pronounced *YOHM-kipper* or *yohm-key-POOR*) follows ten days later. It's a solemn fast day, the sages point out, much like fasting before a wedding.

Five days later comes the seven-day joyous festival of Sukkot. Might this be intentional, some ask, a way to mirror the seven blessings of a typical Jewish wedding ceremony?

After Sukkot are the days of Shemini Atzeret and Simchat Torah. These ecstatic occasions, some are quick to point out, are reminiscent of a married couple happily toasting each other and joyously breaking their wine or champagne glasses before dancing together and consummating their relationship.

Is all this what God had in mind in arranging these holy days as he did? No one can say for sure, but we have to admit, the parallels are intriguing and evocative.[70]

Rosh Hashanah

"Rosh Hashanah is humanity's wake-up call."

—Shmuley Boteach

A Jewish handyman paid an unexpected visit to his rabbi. In a halting voice, the man confessed to having done a shoddy, shady job painting his neighbor's house. He'd charged a premium price—but hadn't bothered to carefully scrape and sand the home's peeling woodwork first. He'd purchased inferior paint—and promptly thinned it with turpentine!

With the Jewish High Holy days fast approaching, the painter begged the rabbi, "What should I do? I feel terrible. How can I atone for my sins?"

The rabbi looked at the guilt-ridden man and smiled. "You know the right thing to do," he said. "Repaint. Repaint and thin no more!"

This old bit of religious humor always elicits more groans than grins, but it gets to the heart of what Rosh Hashanah is all about.

Rosh Hashanah (literal meaning "head of the year") is a designated time of repentance. If that sounds serious, it's because it is. Rosh Hashanah is also known as the Day of Judgment, so we would expect it to be solemn. But Rosh Hashanah is far from grim for at least three reasons. First, it offers a chance for healthy personal introspection and spiritual recommitment. Second, as the official beginning of the Jewish New Year, it signals the opportunity to wipe the slate clean and make a fresh start. Third, according to one Jewish tradition, God created humans on this day. This makes Rosh Hashanah a birthday celebration for humanity. Rabbi Susan Silverman says, "As we do on any birthday, we take stock of the past year, have a party, eat sweet foods, and look forward to a better year."[71]

The Origin of Rosh Hashanah

Here's a fact that shocks some people: the phrase *Rosh Hashanah* is not found in the Torah. It's actually a rabbinical title that dates to around the first or second century CE. The celebration itself, however, is clearly commanded in the Torah: "The LORD spoke to Moses: 'Tell the Israelites: In the seventh month, on the first day of the month, you are to have a day of complete rest, commemoration, and trumpet blasts—a sacred assembly. You must not do any daily work, but you must present a fire offering to the LORD'" (Leviticus 23:23–25, CSB).

Careful readers are now scratching their heads. Why would the Jewish New Year begin on the first day of the *seventh* month?

There's no simple answer to this question. In Exodus 12:2 the Lord tells Moses that the month of Nissan "is to be the beginning of months for you; it is the first month of your year" (CSB). And yet the Jewish year number (Jews refer to 2019–2020 as calendar year 5,779[72]) doesn't change on Nissan 1. It changes on Rosh Hashanah in the seventh Jewish month of Tishrei (i.e., in early autumn). Some believe this is because of the Jewish tradition mentioned above that

 All Those New Years!

The Talmud list four days as being "first days of the year":
- Tishrei 1 (Rosh Hashanah, the beginning of the new *civil* year)
- Shevat 15 (the new year for *trees*)
- Nissan 1 (Passover, the beginning of a new Jewish *festival* year)
- Elul 1 (the new year for determining the *tithing* of cattle)

God created humanity on Tishrei 1. Others say it's because the fall harvest signals the end of one agricultural year and the start of another. Whatever the reason, one fact remains:

 The Jewish Calendar and Gregorian Calendar Compared

Jewish Calendar Month	Gregorian Calendar Equivalent
Tishrei	September/October
Heshvan	October/November
Kislev	November/December
Tevet	December/January
Shevat	January/February
Adar	February/March
Nissan	March/April
Iyar	April/May
Sivan	May/June
Tammuz	June/July
Av	July/August
Elul	August/September

when people speak of the "Jewish New Year," they're referring to Rosh Hashanah.

The Meaning of Rosh Hashanah

Rosh Hashanah, celebrated for two days, ushers in ten consecutive days of penitence, ending with Yom Kippur, Judaism's most sacred observance. Yom Kippur is the day God forgave the Israelites for the sin of worshiping the golden calf and gave Moses the second, permanent tablets (Exodus 34). All together these ten days are known as the Jewish High Holy Days, and they conclude a forty-day period of contrition known as the Yamim Noraim (the "Days of Awe"). Unlike other Jewish holidays that highlight a change in seasons or commemorate events from Israel's history, the High Holy Days have an internal focus: assessing one's relationship with God and renewing one's spiritual devotion.

The Mishnah (sometimes referred to as the Oral Torah—a comprehensive collection of rabbinical teachings on the written Torah) sees Rosh Hashanah primarily as a day of judgment. Jewish tradition says that on this day "three

books are opened" and the fates of all people are determined for the coming year. Individuals regarded by God
as righteous get their names inscribed in the Book of Life.
Those who are clearly wicked are, in the words of Psalm
69:28, "blotted out of the book of the living," and recorded
in the Book of Death. Individuals who are neither holy nor
wicked are given an extension of sorts. They have until Yom
Kippur, the Day of Atonement, to reflect on their ways, repent of their sins, and renew their commitment to God.

The Practices of Rosh Hashanah

Rosh Hashanah services can be lengthy (the morning service lasting five or six hours), because three grand themes
are heavily emphasized. The first theme is *malkiyot*, which
refers to the "kingship" of God. This idea is revealed in
solemn prayers of repentance that "center on the image of
God as Creator, King, and judge, who exercises forgiveness
and compassion toward those who turn to him and seek his
mercy."[73]

A second emphasis is *zikhronot* ("remembrances"). This
aspect of Rosh Hashanah involves the recitation of Jewish

scriptures—for example, the collection of psalms known as the Hallel—that review what God has done in history for his people. God's people not only remember him but also say prayers requesting that he remember them in the New Year.

The third theme is *shofarot*. To outsiders, this repeated blowing of the shofar is easily the most striking and

 What's a Shofar?

A shofar is a ram's horn—although antelope, gazelle, and goat horns are sometimes used too.

Because it was a ram that Abraham sacrificed after God spared his son Isaac—and because Jewish tradition says that this particular ram's horn was blown at Mount Sinai in the giving of the Torah—Jews customarily read the Abraham-Isaac story in Genesis 22 at Rosh Hashanah.

Though shofars sound exotic and rare, they're not hard to find. Online retailers actually sell real shofars from Israel. Expect to pay anywhere between $15 and $200, depending on the size—and whether your order includes a fancy drawstring bag and anti-odor spray.

memorable feature of Rosh Hashanah. It's why the festival is sometimes called the Feast of Trumpets.

Much like an alarm clock jolts you out of a deep sleep or a police siren causes your heart to race, the repeated shofar blasts on Rosh Hashanah (one hundred times in traditional congregations) are intended to echo throughout the synagogue and jar the soul. As the prophet Amos wrote, "If a ram's horn is blown in a city, aren't people afraid?" (Amos 3:6, CSB). The use of the shofar aligns perfectly with what Maimonides said is the essential message of Rosh Hashanah: "Awake, ye sleepers, and ponder your deeds. Remember your Creator, and return to Him in penitence. Be not among those who miss reality in their pursuit of shadows, and waste their years in a quest for vain things. Look to your souls. Examine your acts. Forsake evil . . . so that God may have mercy on you."[74]

Rabbi Irving Greenberg notes how Rosh Hashanah is structured like a trial and says the shofar blast communicates, "Oyez! Oyez! This court is in session! The Right Honorable Judge of the World presiding."[75] The goal of this holy day, however, isn't condemnation. It's to help the Jewish people begin the new year in a state of "personal and collective renewal."[76]

When the shofar sounds, Jews enter a time of rigorous spiritual self-assessment. The ensuing days of penitence are marked by three important words: *teshuvah* (repentance or return), *tefillah* (prayer), and *tzedekah* (charity).

Teshuvah involves taking stock of our lives, considering where we have gone off track and how we have harmed others in the preceding year. Such reflection, to be effective, requires ruthless honesty with oneself. It further requires the humbling, often scary step of approaching those we have wronged and seeking forgiveness. We cannot, of course, *make* others let go of grudges, but Jewish teaching requires that one make at least three attempts to rectify wrongs done to others.

The process is painful, sometimes miserable. Fortunately, at Rosh Hashanah misery not only *loves* company but *gets* company. There is comfort in knowing that everyone in the community is engaging in these humbling exercises of confession and difficult acts of contrition. And really, it's not for God's sake but for our own benefit. As Rabbi Ted Falcon explains, "God already knows everything you could ever confess to, and—incredibly—is already forgiving and merciful. But you can't appreciate that mercy until you open up, examine your life, and work toward making changes."[77]

Tefillah involves reaching up to God, connecting with the Almighty via prayer. In the corporate Rosh Hashanah prayers, the Jewish people acknowledge God as the ruler of the world.

Finally, as part of Rosh Hashanah, participants engage in tzedekah. They make gifts of charity. They do righteous deeds. They recommit themselves to live according to God's commandments. This is because the Bible teaches that true repentance involves more than a fleeting thought of "I should probably try harder." Repentance means changing one's direction, turning back, or returning. Repentance is change; and the proof of repentance, to adapt the old saying, is in the living. Genuinely repentant people inevitably go in new and different ways. They seek out those they have wronged and endeavor to make amends. They forgive their enemies. They help the poor and determine to live in other ways that make the world a better place.

Together these three words—*teshuvah, tefillah,* and *tzedekah*—make up the spirit of Rosh Hashanah. Spiritual renewal for the Jewish New Year involves repentance, prayer, and charity.

 What's Elul?

The entire Jewish month of Elul, just before the Days of Awe (i.e., Rosh Hashanah and Yom Kippur), is viewed by observant Jews as a time of heightened spiritual preparation. Elul is not a holiday in the strict sense of the word, but the month does spark internal reflection.

Except on the Sabbath, the shofar is blown daily during Elul. Psalms of repentance are recited. At the end of the month, Jews seek forgiveness from those they've wronged. They also begin to wish one another *shanna tovah* (a good new year).

Many Jews end Rosh Hashanah by participating in the beautiful ritual of *tashlich* (which means "casting away"). At a nearby body of water (ideally the sea, but rivers, lakes, and streams suffice for those who don't live near an ocean), worshipers cite Micah 7:19, "You will cast all our sins into the depths of the sea," and toss bread crumbs into the water. This dramatic act symbolizes the forgiveness promised by God to those who sincerely repent.

After the Rosh Hashanah services, the happy celebration begins. Celebrants eat circular foods—for example, challah bread baked in a round braid instead of a customary loaf. The different shape symbolizes the cyclical nature of time and how the old year flows into the new. Worshipers also indulge in a whole array of symbolic foods, most famously apples dipped in honey, eaten to symbolize the hope that the upcoming year will be sweet for all. In fact, a common greeting at this holiday is *"Shanah tovah u'metuka,"* which is the wish for "a good and sweet year."

In light of such festivities, the late Gil Marks (a rabbi, chef, and author of five Jewish cookbooks) noted that Rosh

Hashanah, despite its poignancy, is "an occasion of joy and feasting, for in the words of the Talmud, God declares, 'On Rosh Hashanah I look upon all of you as if you had been created for the first time.'"[78]

Sweet new beginnings, all thanks to a gracious God.

Yom Kippur

"Your sins are not so many that you should stay out . . . or so few that you shouldn't come in."

—Synagogue sign on Yom Kippur

In her book *The Alphabet in My Hands*, Marjorie Agosín writes about her memories of Yom Kippur. She explains how she and her mother would dress in white, go down to a nearby riverbank, and gather stones. The two would then toss the rocks into the river:

> We threw the stones into the river with love, stones like prayers. The stones were for our sins, for the times we had disobeyed, been stubborn, wished for bad things to happen. We threw a lot of stones. We

liked the sound they made, and we liked knowing that the turbulent, crystalline river, slippery as bubbles, swept away our sins and evil deeds. Later that afternoon we felt happy and light.[79]

Although perhaps not the most traditional way to mark Yom Kippur, it's hard to think of a better image for the holiday. The heaviness of sin. The lightness of being forgiven.

On the Jewish calendar, Rosh Hashanah and Yom Kippur are distinct. To the Jewish mind, these holy days are inseparable. On Rosh Hashanah, Jews worldwide begin their new year with a rigorous, ten-day process of *teshuvah* (repentance). Then, on Yom Kippur, as Cantor Matt Axelrod paraphrases the Talmud, they "seal the deal."[80]

Yom Kippur means "Day of Atonement." Observant Jews describe it in hushed tones and with reverent phrases like "awe-inspiring," "soul-stirring," "profoundly moving," and "haunting." This day is so sacred that devout Jews simply cannot treat it like any other day. In fact, when the first game of the 1965 World Series fell on Yom Kippur, Sandy

Koufax, the Hall of Fame pitcher for the Los Angeles Dodgers, refused to play.[81]

Even among nonobservant Jews, this particular day resonates deeply. Actor Kirk Douglas said once in an interview, "Throughout my life, when I was moving further and further from Judaism, I always clung to a single thread—Yom Kippur. On that one day, I fasted. I might be shooting it out with Burt Lancaster or John Wayne, but I always fasted."[82]

Perhaps you've heard the old Yiddish wisecrack that any time two Jews get together, there will be at least three opinions? It's true—except when it comes to the subject of Yom Kippur. Jews almost universally recognize Yom Kippur, the "Sabbath of Sabbaths," as the *highest* and *holiest* of Jewish days.

The Origin of Yom Kippur

The Torah tells the remarkable story of Yom Kippur's origin. Working through Moses and a series of inexplicable miracles, God liberated the Hebrew people from slavery in Egypt. They famously traveled through the Red Sea and then gathered at the foot of Mount Sinai. There, the twelve tribes became a nation. They entered into a covenant with God. It was like a marriage, really—God making fabulous promises, the people vowing back, "Everything that the LORD has spoken we will do" (Exodus 19:8).

But when Moses failed to come back down Sinai after the prescribed forty days, the people crafted an idol, a golden calf, and began to worship it. Informed by God of these horrifying events in the valley below, Moses acted decisively: he charged down the mountain, angrily shattered the stone tablets that bore God's commandments, and told the people, "You have sinned a great sin. But now I will go up to the LORD; perhaps I can make atonement for your sin" (Exodus 32:30). With that, Moses again disappeared into the smoke that shrouded Sinai.

When Moses returned, he brought two blessings: (1) the good news that God had forgiven his people and (2) a new set of stone tablets. This took place on the tenth day of the month of Tishrei. Yom Kippur, the Jewish Day of Atonement, has been observed on this day ever since.

The Practices of Yom Kippur

The Torah clearly commands the observance of Yom Kippur. "This shall be an everlasting statute for you, to make atonement for the people of Israel once in the year for all their sins" (Leviticus 16:34).

 The Tallit and Tzitzit

What are those scarf-like coverings Jews wrap themselves in when they pray at religious services? They're prayer shawls, called tallit. Rectangular, and typically made of white silk, linen, or wool, tallit have distinctive stripes (i.e., black or blue threads) running through them. Fringes, or strings called tzitzit (made of the same material), hang from each of the four corners of the tallit.

Some tallit have a blessing embroidered in them—"Blessed are you, O Lord our God, King of the Universe, who has sanctified us with your commandments, and who has commanded us to wrap ourselves in the fringed garments." This is the blessing worshipers say when putting on a prayer shawl.

A few chapters later, more details are given:

> Now, the tenth day of this seventh month is the
> day of atonement; it shall be a holy convocation
> for you: you shall deny yourselves and present the
> Lord's offering by fire; and you shall do no work
> during that entire day; for it is a day of atonement,
> to make atonement on your behalf before the
> Lord your God. For anyone who does not practice
> self-denial during that entire day shall be cut off
> from the people. And anyone who does any work
> during that entire day, such a one I will destroy
> from the midst of the people. You shall do no
> work: it is a statute forever throughout your gener-
> ations in all your settlements. (Leviticus 23:27–31)

The command to "deny yourselves" (or, in some Bible
translations, "afflict your souls") is carried out by Jews
in several ways. Primarily it's by fasting—going without
food or drink. Falcon explains that Yom Kippur is like
"the prayer before the meal" (the meal being the new
year that lies stretched out in front of us): "Just as you

wouldn't eat during a blessing, you don't eat during Yom Kippur."[83]

The devout also avoid sexual relations. They refuse to wear leather shoes. They abstain from bathing and from applying lotions, oils, or cosmetics. The idea behind all these restrictions is to forsake physical comforts and worldly pleasures in order to demonstrate a singular focus on spiritual priorities.

The day before this intense period of self-denial, it is customary to give generously to charity. "To this end, collection boxes called *tzedakah* boxes are found all over . . . in Jewish stores, on the streets of Israel, dug into stone walls of houses or affixed to tree trunks."[84]

Kapparot is a ritual practiced by some Jews in one form or another on the eve of Yom Kippur. The ritual involves waving a live chicken or money over a person's head while reciting a prayer for atonement, after which the value of the chicken, or money itself, is given to the homeless or poor as an act of charity, to atone for one's sins during the previous year.

This symbolic ceremony is meant to stir the emotions toward repentance and is not seen in any way as a form of sacrifice—an act forbidden outside the temple in Jerusalem. Many rabbis discourage the ceremony on several grounds, including animal cruelty.

It is customary to eat a large, joyful meal before the fast begins. In Judaism, fasting means abstaining from both food and water. While there are several "minor" fasts during the year that entail fasting from sunrise to nightfall, there are two "major" fasts, where Jews neither eat nor drink from sunset to the following nightfall, about twenty-five hours. Yom Kippur is a major fast.

If you attend a traditional Yom Kippur service, you will see many in white clothing. Some—certainly the rabbi and cantor—may be dressed in a robe-like garment called a kittel. Many congregants wear rectangular prayer shawls (called tallit) not just during the morning service but for all them.

The holy day actually features five religious services. Depending on the synagogue, these services can look very different.

Just before sundown—and the official beginning of Yom Kippur—Jews participate in the moving Kol Nidrei. Conducted in Aramaic, not Hebrew, this is not so much prayer time as a kind of legal proceeding, a way of releasing worshipers from vows made to God hastily, half-heartedly, or under duress. Against the backdrop of deeply moving music, participants confess their frailty and need for divine grace and mercy. Norman Solomon calls this "one of the most emotionally charged moments of the Jewish year."[85]

 Which Service?

At Yom Kippur Rabbi Kaplan noticed a child staring intently at a large plaque hanging in the lobby of the shul. He approached the boy and said quietly, "G'mar, Tov, Jacob."

"G'mar, Tov, Rabbi," the boy replied, still staring at the long list of names. "Rabbi, what does this plaque mean?"

"It's a memorial, Jacob . . . to all the men and women from our congregation who died in the service."

The boy's eyes widened. After a moment, he gulped and asked, "Which service—the evening or morning?"

Thus begins the evening Ma'ariv service. In it, as in each
Yom Kippur service, participants stand to read the Vidui,
a prayer of confession that lists assorted transgressions.
At the mention of each sin, ardent worshipers beat their
chests.

Because many Jewish holidays *do* feature multiple, often
lengthy services, it can get confusing. Here's what the various services of Yom Kippur are called:

- *Ma'ariv*—an evening service
- *Shakharit*—the morning service
- *Musaf*—an added service (on Shabbat and holi-
  days)
- *Minhah*—an afternoon service
- *Neilah*—the closing prayer service

The Shakharit service follows in the morning, with a
Torah reading from Leviticus about how, on the Day of
Atonement, Israel's high priest was to enter the temple's
Holy of Holies to represent the nation before God. In this
sacred place and during this incredible moment, Jewish
tradition says that the high priest annually did something

no one dared do on any other occasion: he would say the mysterious name of God out loud. Simultaneously, the awestruck Israelites, in order to avoid hearing the shatteringly holy name *of* God, would shout praises *to* God.

In some synagogues, this dramatic scene is reenacted. As the cantor "chants the text describing how the people would fall to the ground, he, too, prostrates himself completely in front of the ark. It's an extremely unusual and compelling moment in the service. It's often misunderstood . . . but this section of the service is really all about the drama. What we modern Jews are trying to do is tap in to that primitive feeling of awe and reverence that our ancestors experienced on Yom Kippur."[86]

Following the lengthy Musaf service, the late afternoon features the Mincha service. During this service, the prophetical book of Jonah is read. Why the curious story about a reluctant prophet who tried to run from God and ended up being swallowed by a great fish? One rabbi explains, "We see Jonah's story as a reminder that we can never flee from God and His judgment, and as an affirmation that He seeks our repentance and longs to forgive us and shower us with His love."[87]

Yom Kippur concludes with the highly charged Neila ("closing") service. Participants here stand and are confronted with the sobering idea that the time for repentance and confession is soon ending and the gates of heaven are about to close. The congregation chants *"Avinu Malkenu"* ("our Father, our King") in unison and listens to a chilling final blast of the shofar.

The Meaning of Yom Kippur

Do you recall the Jewish tradition that says that Rosh Hashanah is a time of divine judgment? That God decides at the start of the new year who will live and who will die? Do you remember the idea that while the wicked are inscribed in the Book of Death and the righteous in the Book of Life, those in between have until Yom Kippur to mend their ways and perhaps affect God's decision? All these weighty realities are an essential part of Yom Kippur. No wonder this Day of Atonement feels so heavy!

Whereas Rosh Hashanah primarily involves making amends and seeking forgiveness from people we have wronged, Yom Kippur is more about showing contrition for our sins against God. We might say the Jewish High Holy Days begin with a horizontal focus—getting right with the people around you—and conclude with a vertical focus—seeking absolution from above. At Yom Kippur, worshipers look up for mercy, even as they continue to honestly and humbly address their failings.

Rabbi Shaul Rosenblatt put it this way: "On Yom Kippur, we stand before God, hand on heart and say, 'God: it's not your fault.' We take responsibility. We are not who we should be, so life is not what it could be. We are the problem in the relationship, not You."[88] But Yom Kippur involves more than parroting mere words and completing a few perfunctory religious rituals. Adherents are expected to do something about their faults. In the words of writer-activist Naomi Wolf, "Every Yom Kippur, Jewish tradition requires a strict spiritual inventory. You aren't supposed to just sit around feeling guilty, but to take action in the real world to set things right."[89]

One rabbi has called Yom Kippur "the great celestial bath, a day in which the sins of the entire nation of Israel are washed away."[90] Others have noted that this "nonstop day of prayer and meditation can rattle and inspire the Jewish soul in a way that no other holiday seems to do."[91]

So what do those rattled and inspired souls do next? They break their fast with a meal. Some then return home and take the first steps on making the sukkah, thus moving "from mitzvah to mitzvah." This signals the approach of the next holiday just ahead on the calendar—Sukkot, the festive occasion during which the Jewish people "camp out" in homemade huts.

HOLIDAYS OF
NATIONAL
SALVATION

The holidays we've considered so far have a strong spiritual, heavenly focus.

But Judaism isn't only about God—it's also about the Jewish people, whom the Bible calls God's "treasured possession" (Deuteronomy 14:2), "a priestly kingdom" (Exodus 19:6), "a people holy to the LORD" (Deuteronomy 7:6), "a people living alone, and not reckoning itself among the nations" (Numbers 23:9).

It shouldn't surprise anyone, then, that two of the most beloved holidays in the Jewish calendar celebrate the miraculous salvation of the Jewish people from the hands of their enemies, albeit in some very different circumstances.

Hanukkah

"What's the best holiday? Hanukkah of course . . . You eat
pancakes every day, spin your dreidel to your heart's content
and from all sides money comes pouring in. What holiday can
be better than that?"

—Sholom Aleichem

(Cited in Philip Goodman, *Rejoice in Thy Festival*)

In late November, Leah impulsively moved. She didn't even consult her family. She hired a couple of cash-strapped college guys with a truck. And in one nippy New York fall day, she managed to get all her belongings into a smaller, slightly less expensive apartment a few blocks south.

After settling in, she called her daughter to make Hanukkah plans.

"Oh, by the way, I forgot to tell you. I downsized."

"You *what*?"

"I moved. Found a nicer place a few streets over."

"Mom! Why didn't you say something? I could have helped."

"I didn't want to bother you."

"*Bother* me? I'm your *daughter*! I would have come."

"What's done is done. Anyway, let me give you directions to my new place. The address is 312 West 46th Street. I'm in apartment 43. In the entryway, you'll see a big panel of buttons. With your elbow, push button 43. I'll buzz you in. Come inside and look for the elevator on your left. Get in, and with your elbow hit the button for the fourth floor. When you get out, go to your left. I'm the third door on the right. Just press the doorbell with your elbow."

"Okay, that sounds easy enough, but why am I hitting all these buttons with my elbow?"

"What?" Leah exclaimed. "You're coming *empty-handed*?"

Hanukkah (pronounced *HAH-nuh-kuh*) is an eight-day celebration marked by food, family, and fun. Don't come empty-handed. And don't expect to leave any other way but full—full of food, of course, but full of hope too.

Hanukkah means "dedication." In fact, it's sometimes referred to as the Feast of Dedication, though more people call it the Festival of Lights.

Hanukkah begins annually on the twenty-fifth day of the Jewish month Kislev (this means it falls occasionally in late November, but usually in December), when the nights are longest. Because of its proximity to Christmas, Hanukkah is often referred to—erroneously—as the "Jewish Christmas." Rabbi Ted Falcon pleads with non-Jews to avoid this description. "Jews have nothing against Christmas, but . . . making the comparison is like saying that Cinco de Mayo is 'the Mexican Mother's Day,' just because these two holidays appear during the same month."[92]

While Christmas celebrates one story—the birth of Jesus—Hanukkah is rooted in two very different stories. One involves a military victory. The other focuses on a miracle.

The Origin of Hanukkah

First things first: Hanukkah *isn't* mentioned in the Jewish Bible (often referred to as the Tanakh; i.e., what Christians call the Old Testament). This is because the events commemorated at Hanukkah took place after all the history recorded in the Jewish Bible. Thus, there's no mention of Hanukkah in the Tanakh.

The holiday's origins are described in the historical books of 1 and 2 Maccabees.[93]

> Now Maccabeus and his followers, the Lord leading them on, recovered the temple and the city; they tore down the altars that had been built in the public square by the foreigners, and . . . purified the sanctuary. . . . It happened that on the same day on which the sanctuary had been profaned by the foreigners, the purification of the sanctuary took place, that is, on the twenty-fifth day of the same month, which was Chislev [Kislev]. They celebrated it for eight days with rejoicing, in the manner of the festival of booths. (2 Maccabees 10:1–6)

This stirring victory of the Maccabees over the occupying Greeks is also described by the first-century Jewish historian Josephus, and there is a brief reference to Hanukkah in the Christian New Testament. In a passage about the life and ministry of Jesus, we read, "At that time the festival of the Dedication took place in Jerusalem. It was winter" (John 10:22).

So, even though we can't find detailed information on Hanukkah in the Bible, other documents from history enable us to piece together the remarkable story. Here's what we know . . .

When Alexander the Great steamrollered through the Near East in the fourth century BCE, Israel was one of the many lands he conquered. Even though the Jewish people were suddenly exposed to Greek culture and ideas, they were permitted to maintain their Jewish identity and lifestyle.

Everything changed when Alexander died. His empire was divvied up, and the Seleucid dynasty assumed control of Israel. In 167 BCE, Antiochus IV Epiphanes (the king of the Seleucid Empire) decided to get tough with his subjects. He demanded—on penalty of death—that the Jewish people renounce their beliefs, abandon their religious practices, and Hellenize (i.e., embrace Greek ideas and behaviors).

Specifically, Antiochus outlawed all things Jewish—the Sabbath, the ritual of circumcision, reading the Torah.

It was when he ordered the Jews to sacrifice unclean swine on assorted Jewish holy altars that an old priest named Mattathias finally said, "Enough!" He and his sons launched a guerilla revolt against the occupying Greeks (and their Jewish sympathizers). So fierce was this family of fighters, they earned the nickname Maccabees, which comes from the Hebrew word for "hammer."

When the Maccabees reclaimed Jerusalem, they purified the temple from its defilement by Antiochus IV and rededicated it to the worship of the God of Abraham, Isaac, and Jacob. Since Antiochus had seized the temple on Kislev 25, Judah Maccabee chose that date in 164 BCE to rededicate it. He then decreed that an eight-day commemoration of this significant event be held annually, beginning on Kislev 25. This is the festival of dedication mentioned in John's Gospel.

In about 500 CE, while commenting on Hanukkah in the Talmud, the Jewish sages made a concerted effort to "rebrand" the holiday. They decided to downplay the role of the "hammering Maccabees" in pushing back the Greeks. Instead they gave the holiday more of a spiritual focus. Here's what the rabbis wrote in the Talmud: "When the Greeks entered the Temple, they defiled all the oils therein, and when the Hasmonean dynasty prevailed against and defeated them, they made search and found only one cruse of oil which lay with the seal of the High Priest, but which contained sufficient [oil] for one day's lighting only; yet a miracle was wrought therein and they lit [the lamp] therewith for eight days."[94]

It's interesting that the books of 1 and 2 Maccabees emphasize the military victory behind Hanukkah. They don't mention any miracles involving oil. But in the Talmud, the military victory gets a sentence and the miraculous oil becomes the star of the show (i.e., God caused oil that was only enough for one night to last eight nights).

The Practices of Hanukkah

Whichever version you adhere to, whatever angle you emphasize, here's what's true: Hanukkah, as it is commonly celebrated today, is an eight-day party. It's a very family-

Menorah or Hanukiah: What's the Difference?

The seven-branched menorah was used only in the temple, and it was lit every day of the year. In the Torah, specific instructions are given as to a menorah's appearance (Exodus 25:31–40; 37:17–24). At Hanukkah, families pull out a special nine-branched candleholder. This special holiday lamp is called a *hanukiah* and comes in all shapes and sizes. Families often have one that is beautifully crafted—perhaps even made of fine silver. They may also have more whimsical hanukiah for each of their children.

A hanukiah has room for eight candles or wicks as well as a slot for a candle or lamp that is different from the others, often in the middle, for the *shammash*, which means "the servant." This means that each of the nights of Hanukkah has its own candle or lamp. The shammash is used to light the actual Hanukkah lights. Part of the ceremony each night of the Festival of Lights is adding an additional candle (moving right to left), then lighting the correct number of candles (left to right).

centered holiday, with more activities taking place in Jewish homes than at the local synagogue.

In keeping with the theme of oil, celebrants eat fried and greasy foods such as fried jelly doughnuts and latkes

 What's a Dreidel?

A popular Hanukkah game for children is playing dreidel (pronounced *DRAY-dull*). A dreidel is a four-sided top, each side sporting one of these four Hebrew letters—Nun, Gimel, Hay, or Shin. Why these four letters, and not one of the other eighteen letters of the Jewish alphabet? Because together these four form an acrostic for the Hebrew phrase *Nes Gadol Haya Sham*, which translates into English as "a great miracle happened there." Interestingly, a dreidel in Israel will be called by its Hebrew name, *sevivon*, and it features different letters: Nun, Gimel, Hay, and Peh (instead of Shin). Why? Because "a great miracle happened HERE" (*Nes Gadol Haya Poh*).

The game is simple to play. Using old buttons, pennies, nuts—or some of the chocolate coins they've (potato pancakes served with applesauce or sour cream). Chocolate "coins" wrapped in gold foil are another common treat.

Over the last hundred years, the giving of real money (called *gelt* in Yiddish) and other gifts has become a more entrenched tradition at Hanukkah. Many Jewish Americans

received as gifts for Hanukkah—players contribute to a "pot." The first player then spins the dreidel. If it stops with the letter Nun ׀ facing up, the spinner gets nothing. If the letter Gimel ג is exposed, the spinner gets the whole pot. If the dreidel shows the letter Hay ה, the player gets half the pot. If it reveals the letter Shin שׁ—or Peh פ—the spinner must add to the pot. Though the game is intended to remind kids of the miracle of Hanukkah, some Jewish parents say the real miracle of dreidel is when their kids get through the game without an argument!

Sometimes active children dispense with wooden tops and play a "human dreidel" version of the game. This involves spinning around madly until they fall down from dizziness. The last child standing wins the game.

are convinced this is due to the holiday's proximity to Christmas. An old *New Yorker* cartoon captures this cultural and religious tension well. It pictures a small Jewish boy wearing a kippah. He's sitting in Santa Claus's lap at the mall. Surrounded by a sea of children, he whispers to Santa, "First of all, this conversation never happened."

Given that the two holidays occur so close together, and that Hanukkah celebrations, like Christmas, include lots of singing, cooking, eating, decorating—and, increasingly—gift giving, the confusion is not hard to understand.

In some homes the books of 1 and 2 Maccabees are read. Some of the stories from these writings are riveting and feature remarkably brave women. In 2 Maccabees we read of a mother and her seven sons. Jewish tradition calls her Hanna, but she is unnamed in the text. The family was captured by the Greeks and ordered to renounce their Jewish faith and eat forbidden pig meat. Rather than obey the evil Antiochus, they all submitted bravely to death.

The Significance of Hanukkah

Hanukkah celebrates light overcoming the darkness. It revels in the miracle of a small amount of oil (enough to light a lamp for only one day) lasting eight days. This fact prompts some to ask, "I understand the miracle of the *final* seven days, but if the Jews had some oil, what was miraculous about the first day of that first Hanukkah?"

One perspective is that the real miracle of Hanukkah was the deep faith demonstrated by the Jews. Realizing they didn't have enough oil for their entire rededication ceremony, they went ahead and lit the menorah anyway. Because of such deep trust in God, they were able to witness God making the oil last far longer than it should have.

Purim

"It is the one day when taking oneself seriously is a sin."
—Rabbi Lawrence Kushner

For most of her life, Abigail Pogrebin's Jewish identity was, in her own words, "a given, not a pursuit." Her family was only semi-observant. They lit candles on Shabbat. Like most

Jews, they attended High Holy Day services and participated in family Passover Seders. At Hanukkah, Abigail's mom—an editor of *Ms.* magazine, which was cofounded by the famous feminist Gloria Steinem—threw outrageous parties.

When Abigail married and had children, she began to wonder more deeply about her faith. This led her to interview more than sixty famous Jews about what being Jewish means. Out of that experience she wrote a book called *Stars of David*. It was her interview with writer Leon Wieseltier that affected her most deeply. He spoke of Jews having a responsibility, a stewardship really, to safeguard the Jewish traditions handed down to them through centuries of hardship. "Do not overthrow the customs that have made it all the way to you," is how he put it. Hearing that, Abigail decided to dive more deeply into her faith.

The result was her becoming bat mitzvah (i.e., a daughter of the commandment)—at age forty! She also found a home synagogue. Then she decided to take an entire year and observe every Jewish holiday on the calendar—

especially the ones she had missed or ignored as a child. From that intense experience came the wise and witty book *My Jewish Year: 18 Holidays, One Wondering Jew.*

Abigail's experience with Purim was especially memorable. She started her celebration by fasting (as Esther, the heroine of the Purim story, did). Later in the day, she delivered batches of *hamantaschen* to various neighbors. Hamantaschen, for the record, is a jelly-filled, tricornered pastry meant to remind celebrants of the three-sided "pirate" hat allegedly worn by Haman, the villain of Purim.

In the afternoon Abigail attended a "Purim Scotch Tasting" at her synagogue, her rabbi serving as the bartender. This is one of the little-known facts of Purim—it involves drinking. *Heavy* drinking. Rabbi Abba ben Joseph bar Ḥama (better known as Rava) says in the Talmud that a person is obligated to become so intoxicated on Purim that he does not know how to distinguish between "Cursed is Haman" and "Blessed is Mordecai." (When one can't tell the difference between the hero and the villain, one is plastered indeed!)

Next Abigail participated in a hilarious reenactment of the Esther-Purim story. Supplied with scripts and ridiculous costumes and props, she and a few other reluctant thespians hammed it up to the delight of the synagogue crowd.

Abigail's conclusion? "This ritual proves that the so-called 'People of the Book' can also be the People of the Party—if only once a year and despite the somber source material. (Haman's plot to annihilate the Jews isn't exactly a laugh riot . . .)"[95]

The Origin of Purim

With its beauty pageants, harems, foiled assassination plots, and genocidal villain, the story of Purim reads less like a sacred Jewish text and more like a best-selling thriller you'd grab at the airport gift shop just before boarding your transatlantic flight.

Good thing we have the exciting book of Esther.

Talk about bleak years. The Jews had been driven from their homeland. The days of big-name prophets like Elijah and

Isaiah were long gone. No one could remember the last time anyone had witnessed a bona fide miracle.

Consequently, two questions hung over the Jews like a cloud: *Has God given up on us? Are we destined to become a forgotten footnote in history?*

Without ever mentioning the name of God, the book of Esther answers both questions with an emphatic *no!* Here's the remarkable story in brief: In the third year of his reign, King Ahasuerus of Persia threw a lavish six-month party to showcase his immense wealth and glory. One night during this prolonged affair, the inebriated ruler ordered his queen, Vashti, to parade (perhaps even scantily clad) in front of his guests. She refused.

The mortified monarch immediately launched a national beauty contest to find a replacement queen. More than three years later, he selected the gorgeous Esther—not knowing she was Jewish. Later, when two royal guards began conspiring to assassinate Ahasuerus, Esther's relative and adoptive father, Mordecai, overheard the men talking and alerted Esther secretly. She told the king, and the plot was foiled.

About the time all these things were happening, Haman, the king's top adviser, somehow convinced his boss to issue an "Everyone Must Bow to Haman" decree. Everyone obeyed this edict—except for Mordecai the Jew.

Haman was so enraged that he formulated a plot to exact revenge on Mordecai and all the Jewish people. Without mentioning Mordecai or the Jews by name, Haman slyly secured the king's approval to carry out a pogrom against all Jews living in the Persian Empire. Haman then cast lots (the Hebrew word is *purim*) to determine the date on which to carry out his deadly plan. The lots announced that Adar 13 would be the day on which the wicked Haman would wipe out the Jewish people. The symbolism here should not be missed. Haman was taunting the Jews, essentially saying, "You think your God is sovereign? In truth, your fate is in the hands of blind chance and my hands."

When Haman's plan became public, Jews everywhere began "fasting and weeping and lamenting" (Esther 4:3). Through a messenger, Mordecai appealed to Queen Esther to intervene with the king to save her people. But Esther was reluctant. So Mordecai bluntly suggested to her that perhaps saving the Jewish people was precisely her mission: "Do not think that because you are in the king's house you alone of all the Jews will escape. For if you remain silent at this time, relief and deliverance for the Jews will arise from another place, but you and your father's family will perish. And who knows but that you have come to your royal position for such a time as this?" (Esther 4:13–14, NIV).

Esther was terrified. Taking the initiative to ask a favor of the world's most powerful man could—and often did—lead to execution! Nevertheless, she asked Mordecai to have all the Jews in Susa fast together with her. Then with a gulp, she said, "I will go to the king, though it is against the law; and if I perish, I perish" (v. 16).

Esther held a private banquet for Ahasuerus and Haman, but she held off making her request. So she invited the

men to join her for a follow-up dinner the next day.
But before the three were able to meet and eat again,
two things happened. First, Haman began building a
gallows for Mordecai. Second, the king developed a case
of insomnia so severe he had to order a servant to come
read to him from the official book of government records
(if *that* can't put a person to sleep, what can?). Wouldn't
you know that the servant *just happened* to read the
record of Mordecai foiling the presidential assassination
plot?

Suddenly Ahasuerus was fully awake. He wanted to know
what had been done to properly honor this man who had
saved his life. When he learned that Mordecai had never
been appreciated, he called for Haman. In one of the best
plot twists ever, the king had his right-hand man, Haman,
put a royal crown and royal robe on Mordecai and parade
him through the streets of Susa on the king's own horse!

Later that day, at Esther's follow-up banquet, the king
discovered that his beloved queen was Jewish—one of
the people Haman was intending to kill. In no time at all,

Haman's genocidal plot was thwarted and he was swinging from the very gallows he had built for Mordecai. What's more, the Jews were authorized by Ahasuerus "to destroy, to kill, and to annihilate any armed force of any people or province that might attack them" (Esther 8:11).

The book of Esther ends with a summary of how Purim became a regular celebration of the Jewish people:

> Haman son of Hammedatha the Agagite, the enemy of all the Jews, had plotted against the Jews to destroy them, and had cast Pur—that is "the lot"—to crush and destroy them; but when Esther came before the king, he gave orders in writing that the wicked plot that he had devised against the Jews should come upon his own head, and that he and his sons should be hanged on the gallows. Therefore these days are called Purim, from the word Pur. Thus because of all that was written in this letter, and of what they had faced in this matter, and of what had happened to them, the Jews established and accepted as a custom for themselves and their

descendants and all who joined them, that without fail they would continue to observe these two days every year, as it was written and at the time appointed. These days should be remembered and kept throughout every generation, in every family, province, and city; and these days of Purim should never fall into disuse among the Jews, nor should the commemoration of these days cease among their descendants.

Queen Esther daughter of Abihail, along with the Jew Mordecai, gave full written authority, confirming this second letter about Purim. Letters were sent wishing peace and security to all the Jews, to the one hundred twenty-seven provinces of the kingdom of Ahasuerus, and giving orders that these days of Purim should be observed at their appointed seasons, as the Jew Mordecai and Queen Esther enjoined on the Jews, just as they had laid down for themselves and for their descendants regulations concerning their fasts and their lamentations. The command of Queen Esther fixed these practices of Purim, and it was recorded in writing. (Esther 9:24–32)

The Practices of Purim

Adar 14, the date set on the Jewish calendar for Purim, falls in late winter (February–March). Perhaps this is why one writer refers to it as "the Jewish equivalent of Mardi Gras, a giddy outburst of energy and excess."[96] It *is* a carnival atmosphere full of feasting (especially on hamantaschen), dressing in wild costumes, laughing raucously, and—for some—the aforementioned heavy drinking.

 Why Purim Is Important for Jews

The importance of Purim for Jews far outweighs the significance of the event in Jewish history [that it commemorates]. The Talmud goes so far as to say, "If all the festivals would pass away, Purim would still be observed."

The story of Purim focuses upon the affairs of the Persian court and the social problems of the empire. God seems to be entirely absent. In fact, His name is not mentioned at all in the book of Esther. Yet, for Jews, this teaches a very important lesson. Jews take Purim as the prime example of God being there behind the scenes and guiding events, even though His presence is not obvious.[97]

Some synagogues read the book of Esther (called *The Megil-lah*) in a more serious manner. Others, as Abigail Pogrebin's experience showed, act it out with comical flourish. It's common during silly Purim plays for adults to boo and for kids to use noisemakers called groggers (or *ra'ashanim* in Hebrew) to drown out the name of the villain Haman every time it is said.

But Purim isn't just a silly celebration. Jews also make charitable gifts based on the command in Esther that rejoicing celebrants should engage in "sending gifts of food to one another and presents to the poor" (Esther 9:22). Some do this for a very practical reason: How can the poor be merry if they don't have the means to celebrate?

The Meaning of Purim

Many people are shocked to discover that the name of God never appears in the biblical story of Esther. The book contains no dramatic "miracles," no plagues falling from heaven on the wicked.

Instead, it shows the Jewish people being delivered from

genocide by a long string of fortunate events. Individually, each of these happenings might be regarded as just a lucky break. But viewed together, in a line, they definitely seem more providential than coincidental. The story of Esther points to the invisible but unmistakable hand of a good and powerful God. The point of Purim is to rejoice in the truth that he is always working behind the scenes, orchestrating events for the benefit of his people.

OTHER HOLIDAYS

Judaism is a *religion of time* aiming at *the sanctification of time.* . . . Most of its observances—the Sabbath, the New Moon, the festivals, the Sabbatical and Jubilee year— depend on a certain hour of the day or season of the year. It is, for example, the evening, morning, or afternoon that brings with it the call to prayer. The main themes of faith lie in the realm of time. We remember the day of the exodus from Egypt, the day when Israel stood at Sinai; and our Messianic hope is the expectation of a day, of the end of days."

—Abraham Joshua Heschel

The Sabbath: Its Meaning for Modern Man

Tisha B'Av

"Panic and pitfall have come upon us,

devastation and destruction.

My eyes flow with rivers of tears

because of the destruction of my people.

My eyes will flow without ceasing,

without respite,

until the LORD *from heaven*

looks down and sees."

—Lamentations 3:47–50

Most of us have anniversaries we dread, dates forever etched in our minds because of loss and grief.

For the Jewish people, however, there's one particular day on the calendar that seems downright cursed—the ninth day of the fifth month. See if you can wrap your mind around the unbelievable flood of national calamities that have occurred throughout Jewish history on this day of Av 9 (Tisha B'Av in Hebrew, pronounced *Teesha beh-AHV*).

The History of Tisha B'Av

To be clear, the Bible never commands a "day of remembrance" on Tisha B'Av. It does, however, describe painful events that took place on that date—and that Jewish tradition says happened on that date.

In the twelfth century BCE, the recently freed Israelites were poised at the edge of the land God had promised their forefather Abraham. But when a reconnaissance team returned with an intimidating report, the people succumbed to fear and refused to enter Canaan. Because of this lapse in faith, God decreed—on Tisha B'Av, according to Jewish tradition—that his people would spend the next forty years wandering in the wilderness (Numbers 13–14; see also the Mishnah, *Taanit* 4:6).

Circa 586 BCE, tragedy struck again. "In the fifth month, on the seventh day of the month—which was the nineteenth year of King Nebuchadnezzar, king of Babylon—Nebuzaradan, the captain of the bodyguard, a servant of the king of Babylon, came to Jerusalem" (2 Kings 25:8). Two days later, on Av 9, the Babylonian commander "burned the house of the LORD, the king's house, and all the houses of Jerusalem; every great house he burned down" (v. 9). Not only was Jerusalem decimated in this invasion, but Solomon's Temple was destroyed and the Jewish people were ripped from their land and taken into exile.

Believe them or not, the rabbis insist that it was also on Ti-sha B'Av in 70 CE when the Romans entered Jerusalem and destroyed Israel's Second Temple. Then, on the same day in 135 CE, the Romans captured the Jewish city of Betar, ef-fectively crushing a revolt led by Simon bar Kokhba, killing untold numbers of Jews, and ultimately plowing over the temple site in Jerusalem.

As Jewish history continued to unfold, this unfortunate day accumulated more and more bitter memories. On Av 9 in 1096 CE, the First Crusade, which resulted in the capture of Jerusalem and the deaths of hundreds of thou-sands of Jews, is said to have begun. On Tisha B'Av in 1290 CE, King Edward issued an edict expelling all Jews from England. On Av 9 in 1492 CE, the Alhambra Decree (of Ferdinand and Isabella) did the same to Jews in Spain. In 1670 CE the Holy Roman Emperor Leopold followed suit, demanding all Jews leave Austria by a deadline of Av 9. On Tisha B'Av in 1914 CE, the Russians mobilized their forces, effectively igniting World War I, which many "be-lieve marked the beginning of the end" for Jews in eastern Europe.[98]

The Practices of Tisha B'Av

After that long, depressing list, is anyone surprised that Av 9, which annually falls between late July and early August, is a national day of mourning for the Jewish people? No weddings or celebratory events of any kind are scheduled. Observant Jews fast for twenty-five hours,[99] just as they do on Yom Kippur. They abstain from pleasurable activities like bathing, washing, shaving, watching TV, and engaging in sexual relations. They refrain from wearing leather shoes (too comfortable) or fancy jewelry (too showy). Even Torah study is frowned upon lest, on a day earmarked for grieving, one experience too much "rejoicing" of the heart (Psalm 19:8).

Services at the synagogue are stripped down, simple, and somber. Some synagogues drape the ark in black. In the evening service, the synagogue cantor quietly and slowly chants the book of Lamentations. This mournful elegy, attributed to the prophet Jeremiah and apparently composed as he witnessed the destruction of Jerusalem and the temple, is deeply moving. It is a requiem, a confession of sin, a plea for God to hear and heal.

In the morning service, worshipers do not wear tefillin or tallit (prayer shawls). They sit low to the ground, on stools, or even on cushions on the floor, as when one sits shiva (i.e., mourning the death of a relative).

 ## Yom HaShoah

Since the end of World War II, many people have wondered why the Holocaust isn't a focus on the Jewish day of mourning that commemorates so many other national calamities.

In 1959, the Israeli government established a special, separate Holocaust remembrance day called Yom HaShoah, which is roughly two weeks after Passover.[100] Because Tisha B'Av has such a temple emphasis, the Knesset (the legislature of Israel) reasoned that a day set apart for commemorating the Holocaust would appeal to more secular Jews.

In Israel on this day, a siren signals a designated time of silence. Motorists stop driving, pull over, and stand at attention to honor the memories of victims.

The Significance of Tisha B'Av

The Bible says there is "a time to weep, and a time to laugh; a time to mourn, and a time to dance" (Ecclesiastes 3:4). Jews laugh and dance at Purim, during Sukkot, during a Simchat Torah celebration, and on lots of other days.

Tisha B'Av is a time for weeping and mourning. Remembering a painful past is never fun, but it is always wise: "Honoring days of sadness reminds you that life is full of ups and downs, and that living fully means taking the bad along with the good."[101]

Tu B'Shevat

"All the trees of the forest sing for joy
before the LORD; for he is coming,
for he is coming to judge the earth.
He will judge the world with righteousness,
and the peoples with his truth."
—Psalm 96:12–13

Jewish mystics like to tell the story of the famed Jewish teacher Honi coming upon a man planting a carob tree.

"How long will it be before that tree bears fruit?" the old scholar inquired.

"At least seventy years," the man replied.

Honi's eyes grew wide. "But you will probably not be alive in seventy years!"

The man shrugged. "I came into a world filled with carob trees. Just as my ancestors planted trees for me to enjoy, so I plant for my descendants."[102]

The Origin of Tu B'Shevat

Who knew that on the Jewish calendar there's a holiday celebrating *trees*? That's right, on the fifteenth day of Shevat (i.e., the Jewish month that coincides with January–February), many Jews, especially in Israel, celebrate a modern holiday popularly known as the "New Year for the Trees."

This kind of "Jewish Arbor Day" serves as the official end of the winter season in Israel and the beginning of spring. It's at this time that the almond trees burst into pink and white blossoms.

Tu B'Shevat (pronounced *too beesh'VAT*) is certainly not a biblically mandated holiday. Yet there is so much in the

Bible about trees, it's not a total surprise that the sages would create a special day to focus on them. The opening pages of the Bible, for example, trace all the troubles of the human race back to the first man and woman eating fruit from a forbidden "tree of the knowledge of good and evil" (Genesis 2:17–3:7). There's also a command in Leviticus 19:23–25 that stipulates when the Israelites plant trees, they are not to eat the fruit of those trees for three years. In the fourth year, any and all fruit is dedicated to God and is not to be eaten. In temple times, this fruit was taken to Jerusalem and offered to God. In the fifth year, harvesters were free to eat.

We can't forget the mitzvah in Deuteronomy that says, "If you besiege a town for a long time, making war against it in order to take it, you must not destroy its trees by wielding an ax against them. Although you may take food from them, you must not cut them down. Are trees in the field human beings that they should come under siege from you?" (20:19).

And how about the psalm cited above that speaks of the trees singing for joy before the Lord when he comes to judge the earth?

Rabbis in Talmudic times saw in all these references the need for a kind of "botanical Rosh Hashanah"—a new year for the plant kingdom.

The Practices of Tu B'Shevat

How is this little-known holiday celebrated?

- *Planting trees*—Many individuals and families use this occasion to engage in reforestation efforts.
- *Supporting conservation efforts*—Gifts of charity (tzedekah) are directed to groups that feed the hungry or to organizations that seek to raise ecological awareness and make the earth—and especially Israel—green.
- *Eating fresh or dried fruit*—This includes dates, raisins, almonds, figs, and carob; some have the custom of a seder Tu b'Shvat, which is eating specific fruits in a particular order and reading biblical and spiritual meanings connected to them.

The Meaning of Tu B'Shevat

On this day, "we return to the place of our first encounter with trees—the Garden of Eden. We enter once again into harmony with nature as we were in the Garden. The antagonism between humans and nature is set aside. . . . We reconnect to . . . the Tree of Life."[103]

GLOSSARY

Amidah "standing"—a collection of prayers and blessings that make up the center part of a religious service

Etrog (plural, *etrogim*)—a large, bright yellow citrus fruit (citron) that is raised, together with the lulav, by worshipers during the Jewish festival of Sukkot

Haggadah (plural *Haggadot*) "telling"—a written liturgy (or order of service) containing texts, prayers, and blessings for recitation during the Passover meal or Seder

Halakhah—Jewish law

Hametz—leaven or any food with leaven in it; forbidden at Passover

Hanukiah—a special nine-branched menorah (candelabra) used at Hanukkah

Havdalah—the concluding ceremony of a Jewish Sabbath ceremony that signals the official beginning of a new week

Hiddur Mitzvah "beautification of the commandment"— the practice of using beautiful articles and religious implements in Jewish services and celebrations

Kiddush "making holy"—a blessing of consecration recited on Shabbat and holidays over wine

Kippah—a round cap worn to honor God; in Yiddish, referred to as a yarmulke

Kittel—a white robe worn by a rabbi or cantor (or others) at Yom Kippur and on other sacred occasions

Kosher "proper" or "fit"—used most often in reference to foods that conform to Jewish law

Lulav—a bouquet or bundle of willow, myrtle, and palm branches that is raised and waved or shaken at Sukkot celebrations

Megillah "scroll"—most commonly used in reference to the scroll of Esther (which is read at Purim)

Mitzvah—a commandment, commanded deed, or good deed

Shabbat—the origin of the English word Sabbath; in Yiddish, *Shabbos*

Shofar—a primitive, hollowed-out ram's horn, though sometimes from an antelope or gazelle, used to sound warnings or summon people

Shul—the Yiddish word for synagogue (Hebrew, *Beit Knesset*)

Sukkah (plural *sukkot*)—a homemade hut or temporary dwelling inhabited by families during the Jewish festival of Sukkot each fall

Tallit—a prayer shawl worn during synagogue services

Talmud—a massive compilation of rabbinical interpretations and commentary on the Torah

Tanakh—the Jewish Bible; the name is derived from an acrostic for the three broad sections of biblical books: the Torah, the Nevi'im (prophets), and Ketuvim (writings)

Tefillin—another name for phylacteries, the leather straps and boxes worn by observant Jews on the arm and forehead during weekday morning services in obedience to the Torah command of Deuteronomy 6:8

Teshuvah "repentance"

Tikkun Olam "repair the world"—a Jewish imperative to make a positive difference in the world

Tzedekah—gifts of charity

Tzitzit—the fringy threads on the four corners of a prayer shawl (tallit)

Yiddish—the language (a combination of Hebrew and early German) spoken by Jews of European descent

Yizkor—a memorial service for the dead that is recited at the three festivals and Yom Kippur

NOTES

[1] The Torah, or Pentateuch, is the collective name for the first five books (i.e., the first major section) of the Jewish Bible. The other sections of the Jewish Bible are the Nevi'im (the prophets) and the Ketuvim (the writings). Together these three sections are often called the Tanakh, which is actually an acrostic formed by the first letters—*T*, *N*, *K*—of the names of the three sections. What Jews call the Bible or the Tanakh, Christians refer to as the Old Testament.

[2] The biblical term *moed*—usually translated simply as "festival"—actually means "meeting" or "appointed time" or "meeting time."

[3] In this book we will use the word *holiday*, but mostly in the old, original sense of "holy day."

[4] Meyerhoff Center for Jewish Studies, "Mitzvot and Art: What Is the Connection?," Sefaria, https://www.sefaria.org/sheets/11081.

[5] Rabbi Noah Weinberg, "Shabbat: Heaven on Earth," aish.com, May 15, 2004, http://www.aish.com/sh/t/e/Shabbat_-_Heaven_on_Earth.html.

[6] Hayim Halevy Donin, *To Be a Jew* (New York: Basic Books, 1972), 61.

[7] Lawrence Kushner, *The Way into Jewish Mystical Tradition* (Woodstock, VT: Jewish Lights Publishing, 2001), 144.

[8] Lynne M. Baab, *Sabbath Keeping* (Downer's Grove, IL: InterVarsity Press, 2005), 26.

[9] Ibid., 27.

[10] There are several competing ideas about what *manna* means. Some believe it means "what is it?" based on a theory about the Egyptian word *mon*.

[11] Norman Solomon, *Judaism: A Very Short Introduction* (Oxford: Oxford University Press, 1996), 55.

[12] Nan Fink, *Stranger in the Midst: A Memoir of Spiritual Discovery* (New York: Basic Books, 1997), 96.

[13] Ted Falcon and David Blatner, *Judaism for Dummies* (Hoboken, NJ: John Wiley & Sons, Inc., 2013), 237.

[14] Yitzchok Adlerstein, "A Weekly Trip to Hawaii," Jewish Action, https://jewishaction.com/religion/shabbat-holidays/a-weekly-trip-to-hawaii/.

[15] Abraham Joshua Heschel, *The Sabbath: Its Meaning for Modern Man* (New York: Farrar, Straus and Giroux, 1951), 10.

[16] Harold S. Kushner, *To Life! A Celebration of Jewish Being and Thinking* (New York: Warner Books, 1993), 99–100.

[17] Donin, 64.

[18] Anita Diamant and Howard Cooper, *Living a Jewish Life* (New York: HarperCollins, 1991), 41.

[19] Norman Lamm, "Sabbath Rest," in *Yavneh Shiron*, ed. Eugene Fink and Tom Ackerman (New York: Yavneh, 1969), 43.

[20] Irving Greenberg, *The Jewish Way: Living the Holidays* (New York: Summit Books, 1988), 139.

[21] Ibid., 131.

[22] Cited in Elliot Kiba Ginsburg, *The Sabbath in the Classical Kabbalah* (Albany, NY: State University of New York Press, 1989), 88.

[23] The Bible mobilizes a special word for the kind of activity prohibited on Shabbat. This word is better translated "creative labor" (*melacha*) than "work" (*avodah*). But the question is, what qualifies as "creative labor"? Though the Bible gives only a general prohibition against work, the Mishna (a massive collection of biblical commentaries and interpretations by respected Jewish rabbis compiled about 200 CE) spells out thirty-nine categories of creative labor that are forbidden. These include such activities as baking, plowing, tying (or untying) a knot, sewing, catching game, hammering, transporting objects, etc. These activities are understood to have been part of building the mishkan, the desert tabernacle.

[24] Jews from Eastern Europe might call a container like this a pushke, from the Polish word for "can."

[25] Diamant and Cooper, 43.

[26] Talmud (Pirke Avot 3:17).

[27] Made from all kinds of materials (e.g., tin, wood, silver, porcelain, etc.), spice boxes frequently resemble towers, but come in numerous other shapes and forms. Many are precious family heirlooms.

[28] Gabriella Auspitz Labson, *My Righteous Gentile: Lord Wedgwood and Other Memories* (Jersey City, NJ: KTAV Publishing House, 2004), 11–12.

[29] Cited in Berel Wein, "A Passover Message from an Unexpected Source: Ben Gurion's Speech at the Peel Commission," Jewish History (blog), March 24, 2010, https://www.jewishhistory.org/ben-gurion-peel-commission/.

[30] Cited in Baruch M. Bokser, *The Origins of the Seder: The Passover Rite and Early Rabbinic Judaism* (Berkeley: University of California Press, 1984), 82.

[31] Cited by Steven J. Rubin, Ed., in *Celebrating the Jewish Holidays: Poems, Stories, Essays* (Hanover, NH: Brandeis University Press, 2003), 339.

[32] *Pesach Haggadah* (Magid: Rabban Gamliel's Three Things). For full text see https://www.sefaria.org/Pesach_Haggadah%2C_Magid%2C_Rabban_Gamliel's_Three_Things?lang=bi.

[33] Falcon and Blatner, 307.

[34] *Bubbe* is the Yiddish word for "grandmother."

[35] *Balabusta* is Yiddish for "mistress of the house" or "homemaker."

[36] Mayim Bialik, "Cleaning for Passover, Missing My Bubbe," kveller.com, March 26, 2012, https://www.kveller.com/cleaning-for-passover-missing-my-bubbe/.

[37] Michael Strassfeld, *The Jewish Holidays: A Guide and Commentary* (New York: Harper & Row Publishers, 1985), 9.

[38] Ashkenazic Jews are those with roots in Germany, France, and Eastern Europe.

[39] Sephardic Jews are those originating from Spain, Portugal, North Africa, and the Middle East.

[40] Diamant and Cooper, 215.

[41] *Stuff Jews Should Know podcast*, "What Is Passover Seder?," March 22, 2013.

[42] Yaffa Eliach, *Hasidic Tales of the Holocaust* (New York: Oxford University Press, 1982), 16–19.

[43] Matt Axelrod, *Your Guide to the Jewish Holidays: From Shofar to Seder* (Lanham, MD: Jason Aronson, 2014), 135.

[44] *Lag* is the number 33. Hebrew letters correspond to numbers, such that *lamed* is 30 and *gimel* is 3. *Lag ba'Omer* is thus the 33rd day of counting the Omer.

[45] Axelrod, 135.

[46] Midrash (Shir HaShirim Rabbah 1:12). For full text see https://www.sefaria.org/Shir_HaShirim_Rabbah.1.1?lang=bi.

[47] Diamant and Cooper, 234.

[48] Strassfeld, 80.

[49] Abigail Pogrebin, *My Jewish Year: 18 Holidays, One Wondering Jew* (Bedford, NY: Fig Tree Books, 2017), loc. 3910–13, Kindle.

[50] Strassfeld, 82.

[51] Jane Kaufman, "Sukkot Imbued with Mystery, Mysticism, Memories," Masslive.com, September 17, 2013, https://www.masslive.com/living/index.ssf/2013/09/jane_kaufman_sukkot_imbued_with_mystery_mysticism_memories.html.

[52] Falcon and Blatner, 272.

[53] Greenberg, 97.

[54] Strassfeld, 126.

[55] Ibid., 128.

[56] Axelrod, 44.

[57] Isidor Margolis and Sidney L. Markowitz, *Jewish Holidays and Festivals: A Young Person's Guide to the Stories, Practices, and Prayers of Jewish Celebrations* (New York: Citadel Press, 1995), 44.

[58] Talmud (Sukkah 51b). For full text see https://www.sefaria.org/Sukkah.51b?lang=bi.

[59] Ellen Frankel and Betsy Platkin Teutsch, *The Encyclopedia of Jewish Symbols* (Northvale, NJ: Aronson, 1992), 165.

[60] Strassfeld, 14.

[61] Shmuley Boteach, *Judaism for Everyone* (New York: Basic Books, 2009), 368–69.

[62] Axelrod, 57.

[63] A. J. Jacobs, *The Year of Living Biblically* (New York: Simon & Schuster, 2007), 86.

[64] Strassfeld, 71.

[65] In addition to Shemini Atzeret, Yizkor is also said as a community at Yom Kippur, Passover, and Shavuot.

[66] Talmud (Pirkei Avot 5:22); see https://torah.org/learning/pirkei-avos-chapter5-26/.

[67] Solomon, 58.

[68] Dovid Rosenfeld, "Simchat Torah: Just You and Me," Aish.com, September 17, 2013, http://www.aish.com/h/su/saast/Simchat-Torah-Just-You-and-Me.html.

[69] Axelrod, 71.

[70] Ronald L. Eisenberg, *The JPS Guide to Jewish Tradition* (Philadelphia: The Jewish Publication Society, 2004), 228.

[71] Yosef I. Abramowitz and Rabbi Susan Silverman, *Jewish Family & Life* (New York: Golden Books, 1997), 142.

[72] Year 1 of the Jewish calendar coincides with the creation of the world. Using the genealogies in the Bible, Jewish tradition sets that date at 3,761 years before the Common Era. Therefore, one can calculate the current "Jewish year" by adding 3,760 to the current year of the Gregorian calendar. What most of the world considers the year 2019 is the year 5,789 for Jewish people.

[73] Solomon, 62.

[74] Mishneh Torah (Laws of Repentance 3:4). For full text see https://www.sefaria.org/texts/Halakhah/Mishneh%20Torah.

[75] Greenberg, 195.

[76] Boteach, 350.

[77] Falcon and Blatner, 251.

[78] Gil Marks, *The World of Jewish Entertaining* (New York: Simon & Schuster, 1998), 82.

[79] Rubin, 185.

[80] Axelrod, 26.

[81] The Minnesota Twins won the game handily. Koufax did, however, pitch in three subsequent games of the series. He tossed two shutouts, led the Dodgers to the championship, and won the series' Most Valuable Player award. In 1972, at age thirty-six, Koufax became the youngest player ever elected to the Baseball Hall of Fame.

[82] Jenni Frazer, "Kirk Douglas: The Quintessential Tough Guy Reaches 100," *The JC*, December 8, 2016, https://www.thejc.com/culture/film/profile-kirk-douglas-at-100-1.428885.

[83] Falcon and Blatner, 264.

[84] Marc-Alain Ouaknin, *Symbols of Judaism* (New York: Assouline Publishing, 2000), 70.

[85] Solomon, 63.

[86] Axelrod, 40.

[87] Yechiel Eckstein, *Holy Days of Israel* (Chicago: The International Fellowship of Christians and Jews, 2011), 84.

[88] Shaul Rosenblatt, "Yom Kippur: A Day of Reconciliation," Aish.com, September 10, 2007, http://www.aish.com/h/hh/yom-kippur/theme/48970706.html.

[89] Naomi Wolf, "The Silent Treatment," *New York Magazine*, March 1, 2004, https://nymag.com/nymetro/news/features/n_9932/.

[90] Boteach, 354.

[91] Falcon and Blatner, 261.

[92] Falcon and Blatner, 281.

[93] The Apocrypha (the word means "hidden") is a group of ancient Jewish texts considered important but not part of the Jewish Bible. Because these books do appear in the Septuagint—the earliest Greek translation of the Old Testament—some Christian traditions consider them to be sacred scripture.

[94] Babylonian Talmud (Shabbat 21b, Soncino translation). Cited at http://thetorah.com/uncovering-the-truth-about-chanukah/.

[95] Pogrebin, loc. 2680–82.

[96] Diamant and Cooper, 211.

[97] Arye Forta, *Judaism* (Oxford: Heinemann Educational, 1989), 59.

[98] Falcon and Blatner, 346.

[99] From just before sundown on Av 8 to dark on Av 9.

[100] In 1959, the Israeli Knesset officially set Yom HaShoah on Nissan 27, the anniversary of the Warsaw Ghetto Uprising. This brave resistance campaign involved a few poorly armed Jews engaging in guerilla attacks. The Nazis crushed it and intensified their campaign of deporting Jews to the death camps.

[101] Falcon and Blatner, 346.

[102] Adapted from the Talmud (Ta'anit 23a). For full text see https://www.sefaria.org/Taanit.23a?lang=bi.

[103] Strassfeld, 185.

ABOUT
THE AUTHOR

DR. FAYDRA SHAPIRO is a specialist in contemporary Jewish-Christian relations, with a focus on evangelical Christian-Jewish relations. She has published and presented extensively on the topic of Christian Zionism and evangelical Christian support for Israel. Dr. Shapiro's most recent book (2016) is *Christian Zionism: Navigating the Jewish-Christian Border.* She received her PhD in 2000, and her first book received a National Jewish Book Award (2006). Dr. Shapiro is the founding director of the Israel Center for Jewish-Christian Relations. She is also a senior fellow at the Philos Project and a research fellow at the Center for the Study of Religion at Tel Hai College. Prior to making aliyah to Israel, Dr. Shapiro was a university professor for over a decade in a department of Religion and Culture in Canada. A dynamic speaker with extensive experience teaching both Christians about Judaism and Jews about Christianity, Faydra is proud to live in the Galilee area with her family.